The Capitalis... ⌣ —

and the fatal flaws of socialism

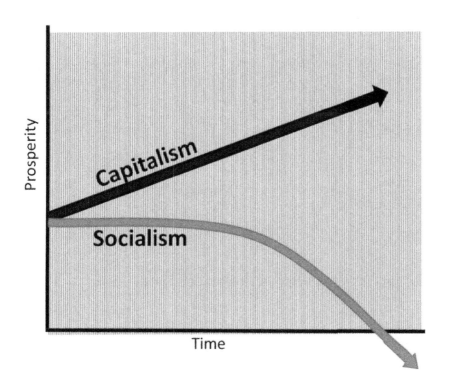

C. Paul Smith

Cover design by Julie Francis

Library of Congress Cataloging in Publication Data

Smith, C. Paul, 1951 –

    The Capitalism Argument—and the fatal flaws of Socialism

    Political and economic commentary and index

International Standard book Number: 9781698685380
Frederick Printing, Frederick, Maryland 21701
Printed in the United States of America
4/20

The Capitalism Argument

TABLE OF CONTENTS

CHAPTER ONE

SOCIALISM ONSLAUGHT THREATENS FREEDOM

Many Americans today do not understand the genius of capitalism. They never learned at school how the capitalism/free enterprise system has been the catalyst and foundation that has made America the most prosperous nation in the history of the world. Failure to understand how capitalism is a key ingredient of our creative, ingenious, productive and prosperous economy puts Americans and their elected officials at risk to mishandle the many political issues that affect our economy. This book is written to help cure this lack of understanding.

The overt campaigning for socialism in America in 2019 in the Presidential nomination process is reason for great alarm among freedom-loving Americans. Socialism is the evil twin of communism. They both share the economic and political philosophies and goals to eliminate private property and individual liberty, and to establish a government-controlled economy and society. Socialism is a fraud. It promises equality and prosperity for all, at the expense of the wealthy (whose riches are to be taken and given to the poor and middle classes). This equality of benefits approach is touted as the new standard of morality which will lead to prosperity and freedom for all. But it is a lie. It may lead to some short-term equality of property holdings, but it invariably leads to a disintegration of the economy and financial ruin for all, while at the same time bringing a loss of freedom for the citizens.

I am writing this because many people do not understand the fatal flaws of socialism. I wish to help inform those whose education is

1

lacking in this matter, so that they will not be deceived—so that they will understand the serious problems of socialism, and so that they will begin to see how socialism has already crept into America's free enterprise economy, and that our freedoms, including our free economy, are at risk to be lost if we abandon capitalism.

President Trump stated in his 2019 State of the Union address that "America will never be a socialist country." I suppose President Trump is expressing his determination to maintain the private ownership of property aspect. I hope that we do preserve what's left of our capitalism, but the nation is already substantially socialist. The fact is that there are already so many elements of socialism in our federal and state governments that America is close to becoming a full-fledged socialist nation.

This highlights several current battles taking place in America. First, in the summer of 2019 there were two dozen Democrat candidates for President who campaigned for remaking American into a socialist nation. Second, our public schools and colleges continually teach our children the virtues and advantages of socialism and sometimes even a hatred for capitalism. Third, America has become increasingly socialist during the past century. And, fourth, the American press and media have become a vocal and powerful force to vilify the American free enterprise system and to proclaim the moral superiority of socialism. The fact that all four of these forces are combining at the same time is proof that capitalism and the free enterprise system are in serious jeopardy in America. The very foundation of liberty in America is under attack, such that there is a grave and present danger that America will embrace even more socialism, until the fundamentals of freedom in America are destroyed from within. Then America will reap the fruits of socialism as she crumbles in the mirage of socialistic prosperity.

This book is written to warn people of the inherent flaws, weaknesses, deceptions and evils of socialism. Capitalism and the free enterprise system is the antidote and the antithesis of socialism. Capitalism is frequently condemned in our public education system and many universities and by political aspirants. But capitalism is not evil, rather it represents the opportunity and incentive that has made America the greatest nation of liberty and prosperity on the face of the earth. And while there will always be examples of capitalists who have been greedy and have taken advantage of the poor, it is nevertheless the universal opportunity that capitalism gives to everyone to succeed and to receive the rewards of one's own ingenuity and hard work that is the foundation of liberty and prosperity in America.

If America continues to destroy the fundamentals of prosperity by following after the socialism mirage of nirvana, then the free enterprise system will be dismantled, and control of private property will be turned over to the state, and economic ruin will ensue. That is why the dream that socialism always promises is just a mirage; no socialistic government has ever brought a nation to prosperity. Just the opposite— socialism always makes an economy worse, and socialism always ends in economic ruin. Even a quick review of historical examples supports this: The Soviet Union, Cuba, and most recently, Venezuela.

Nevertheless, America's mainstream media and many of America's educators insist that socialism is the better way and the right way. And today, in 2019, the socialists have become so emboldened that they openly proclaim that socialism is superior to the capitalism-free enterprise system. This battle is currently being show-cased in the battle for who will be the Democrat Party's nominee for President of the United States. Among the initial two dozen candidates, at least two-thirds of them have been campaigning for more socialism.[1] Bernie Sanders has won the substantive debate within the Democrat Party, for most of the candidates now endorse his views supporting socialism. But, unfortunately for Bernie, I don't think he will end up being the party's nominee. Joe Biden is currently clinging to a slight lead in the polls among the two dozen candidates, but he has been shifting some of his own positions and policies to line himself up with the socialists. This is scary! Will the entire Democrat Party turn to socialism? Some of the

---

[1] Of the initial 26 Democrat candidates for President, those who did not appear to embrace socialism would be former Vice President Joe Biden, Sen. Michael Bennet (CO), former Rep. John Delaney (MD), and former Gov. John Hickenlooper (CO). But the following candidates supported socialism either directly or indirectly: Sen. Cory Booker (NJ), Gov. Steve Bullock (Montana), Mayor Pete Buttigieg (South Bend, IN), former Sec. of Housing, Julian Castro (also former Mayor of San Antonio), Mayor Bill de Blasio (NY), Rep. Tulsi Gabbard (HI), Sen. Kirsten Gillibrand (NY), Sen. Kamala Harris (CA), Gov. Jay Insee (WA), Sen. Amy Klobuchar (MN), Mayor Wayne Messam (FL), Rep. Seth Moulton (MA), Richard Ojeda, Beto O'Rourke (former Rep.-TX), Rep. Tim Ryan (OH), Sen. Bernie Sanders (VT), Joe Sestak (former Rep. PA),Tom Steyer, Rep. Eric Swalwell (CA), Sen. Elizabeth Warren (MA), Marianne Williamson and Andrew Yang.

current Democrat challengers claim they are capitalists and not socialists, but their proposals reveal them clearly to be socialists.[2]

Right before our eyes the Democrat Party is capitulating to the demands of the socialists that are taking over their party. The 2019 contest between the socialists in the Democrat Party is partly remarkable and partly horrifying. In the contestants' zeal to promise equality of bounteous benefits to the broad base of victims from whom they seek support, the socialists overtly promise to do the very things that will undermine the foundations of both freedom and prosperity: Their ephemeral formula is not to urge their followers to be creative, work hard, take initiative, and work with others to reach their realistic dreams. No. Instead, their appeal to voters is: "Ask what your country can do for you!" Their formula is to make the rich share more of their wealth with others. Their formula is to insist that everyone is entitled to the wealth possessed by others. They insist that the people have the right to free stuff from the government—food, housing, health care, education, a living wage, vacation and retirement.

I mentioned that historically prosperity has never been achieved through socialism—so there is no historical precedent that supports the viability of socialism. But let me tell you the reasons why socialism never works. It is true that a government can be empowered to take from the rich and spread it among other citizens. And it is theoretically possible to achieve an initial, general economic equality by so-doing. But two other factors always prevent socialism from leading to utopia—the greed of the leaders, and the destruction of freedom of opportunity. The greed of the leaders is always visible in socialist countries. While socialist policies empower the leaders to take from the wealthy, the leaders always seem to accumulate more than their fair share. And even more importantly, anytime a government takes away property from those who create it through their creativity, incentive, hard work, marketing skills, and management abilities—this stifles and kills the liberties and incentives that create wealth. Socialism kills the very intangibles that are the foundation of wealth and prosperity. That is why, as Prime Minister Margaret Thatcher said: "The problem with socialism is that you eventually run out of other peoples' money."

One interesting aspect of the socialists' rhetoric is that they invariably insist that their philosophy is morally superior to capitalism.

---

[2] Jeanine Pirro, *Radicals, Resistance and Revenge—The Left's Plot to Remake America* (New York: Center Street, 2019), p. 216.

4

At the same time, they label capitalists as greedy and selfish oppressors. Therefore, they also insist that those who support capitalism are also evil. And then they often extend their arguments even further, insisting that because the capitalists are evil oppressors it is therefore just and moral to deny them the right to speak, even if it requires violence, fighting and rioting to prevent capitalists from speaking. All the while these socialist extremists insist that they fully support the First Amendment freedoms of speech and press. For those who are paying attention to the national news in America during the past few years (2015-2019), there are multiple examples of this. Thus, what is unfolding (primarily in the Democrat Party) is an emboldened bunch of economic revolutionaries whose views about socialism are wrong, but who insist their views are best, and who then double down and assert that whoever does not agree with them is evil and unworthy of the constitutional protections of speech and press and protection from unprovoked violence. Some recent examples of this include Google's blocking conservative communications from its search engine; Twitter doing the same thing; and Hollywood socialist elites calling conservatives evil and encouraging the blacklisting of conservative actors.

Every day new followers are ensnared by socialism's euphoric-sounding promises. But those who are hard workers and disciplined thinkers are not taken in by the nice-sounding, but false promises. Socialism is just like the quest for economic security by playing the lottery. Theoretically, the lottery always ensures that 99% of the participants lose, and only a small percentage win the prize. Just as the lottery actually ensures that 99% of the participants fail, so does socialism. Theoretically it fails; historically it has always failed; and it will always fail in the future because it is based upon false and flawed principles. It is superficially appealing to the lazy, but it is rejected by people of vision, insight and discipline.

Nevertheless, socialism continues to find new adherents and proponents in every generation. It has historically been the motivation for political power that has encouraged socialist leaders, as those who are skilled in communication are able to gather followers who will praise them and pay them money for their campaigns. Like the pied-piper who led the children astray, so today, the socialist pied pipers are proving very effective in gathering ignorant masses who blindly embrace the false and destructive notions of socialism.

Thus, socialism must be confronted, exposed and defeated. It will lead to no good. It will actually bring about economic decline at the same time its methods will eliminate liberties that are protected under the U. S. Constitution. That is why it is critical that we understand what socialism is, and that it is based upon false theories and evil forces.

While America is not a totally socialistic nation, it has nevertheless developed into a government that is in large part socialistic. The most recent and major move towards socialism occurred when in 2010 President Obama signed into law the Affordable Care Act. This took one-sixth of our economy and converted the nation's health care industry into a government-run business. This was added to: (a) Social Security and other "New Deal" programs that began in the 1930s; (b) Medicaid, Medicare and Head Start and other "Great Society" programs that began in the 1960s; and (c) other federal socialistic government programs that have come with passage of powerful environmental laws, including the Clean Water Act in 1972, and creation of the Environmental Protection Agency (EPA) in 1970. Although its massive regulations ostensibly pertain only to environmental matters, the fact is that we have found out that virtually every aspect of life has been interpreted to have environmental implications.

Regarding environmental laws, the EPA has come to be one of the largest and most powerful federal agencies—virtually every aspect of our lives has come to be regulated in whole or in part by environmental laws and regulations. On the one hand, you would think that this has nothing to do with socialism. But in fact, the broad philosophical goals of protecting the environment have become so extensive that environmental concerns, including unscientific extremist fears, have come to take over many governmental and political movements. Thus, while environmental concerns may seem unrelated to socialism, yet in practice environmental protection has become one of the primary power arms of socialism.

The "Green New Deal" that was introduced by socialist Democrats in 2019 is a perfect example of this.[3] It is a combination of

---

[3] The "Green New Deal" was proposed in 2019 in the House of Representatives by freshman Congresswoman Alexandria Ocasio-Cortez (D-NY). The Senate version of the bill was introduced by Sen. Ed Markey (D-MA). The bill addresses climate change and economic inequality. Its measures were so extreme and unreasonable that it was soundly repudiated in an early vote in the Senate (0-57). In the Senate vote, many of the Democrats voted "Present" rather than to cast a vote against it.

environmental and other socialist proposals that call for more government control over individuals and their property. And lest you may doubt me on this, you need look no further than the title to the popular environmentalist book by Naomi Klein, *This Changes Everything—Capitalism vs. The Climate* (New York: Simon & Schuster, 2014). Those who advance extreme environmental policies today are invariably opposed to capitalism. There is no better example of this than the "Youth Climate Strike" demonstrations that took place around the world on September 20, 2019. Even a casual observer could not help but see the many anti-capitalist banners that said things like: "Capitalism is evil," and "Save the planet from capitalism."

To socialists, capitalism is the enemy of and the cause of climate change. As Klein writes on the back cover of her book, "The really inconvenient truth is that it's not about carbon—it's about capitalism. The convenient truth is that we can seize this existential crisis to transform our failed economic system and build something radically better." Thus, for Ms. Klein and the environmentalists, socialism is the way to fix climate change; for them, when the government controls everything, the government can make people do the things that will stop climate change.

America's rising generation that now embraces socialism is typically ignorant of important historical matters. For example, they seem ignorant of the battle against socialism that was a key part of the conflict with the Third Reich in World War II. When America and Great Britain were fighting against the Nazis' socialistic regime we were fighting against socialism. Socialism was one of the principal evils against which the U. S. and Britain were fighting.

I am not an economist, and I don't presume to have addressed all the issues and arguments that an economist might make. I am aware, however, that the relative advantages and disadvantages of both capitalism and socialism have been extensively debated by economists for over a hundred years. And this debate regularly occurs in Congress. The national outcome of this debate will be determined by politicians, not economists. This being the case, it is not only appropriate but is essential that ordinary folk be informed of the philosophical foundations of both capitalism and socialism, so that the superiority of free-market capitalism can be made known to as many as possible.

Following the economic crash of 2008, some have postulated that it was a "failure of capitalism" that led to the national recession. (See, e.g., Richard A. Posner, *A Failure of Capitalism* (Cambridge, MA: Harvard University Press, 2009).) But some experts disagree with this view. It is not capitalism that has failed, but the principal problems that led to the market crash and the financial failures were unsound and flawed governmental laws, regulations and policies. There will always be periods of recession in a free-market economy, but in the long run the free market economy will recover and do well. That is what happened after the 2008 crisis. And today, 2019, the stock market and the national economy has made a full recovery; the stock market is at an all-time high, and unemployment is at the lowest it's been in fifty years. Thus, the 2008 crash was not proof of a failure of capitalism, but rather proved that flawed governmental interference in the free market causes more problems than it solves. Posner concludes that "our financial markets need to be more heavily regulated" (Posner, back cover). I would just point out that increased regulation is not the only solution to defective regulations. Sometimes less regulation is better. And it is certainly true that a reduction in the burden of taxes, fees and regulations can often help our economy to be more prosperous. Overall, the recovery of our economy after 2008 shows the soundness and resilience of capitalism.

Is there a need for a book on socialism in 2020? Yes. There are some excellent books written in the 1960s that treat this subject. But now, fifty years later, those messages need to be resurrected, repeated, recognized, and reinforced. Two books that should still be read and studied today are W. Cleon Skousen's, *The Naked Communist*, and Ezra Taft Benson's, *"An Enemy Has Done This."* They support and reinforce the messages of this book. I will make reference to both of these books many times. Nevertheless, there is also a need for a contemporary book that discusses our current situation and reinforces the concerns that Skousen and Benson addressed so effectively fifty years ago. The contribution of this book is to show how the threat of socialism continues to be real and substantial. It is important that we understand the fatal flaws in the multiple proposals of today's socialist candidates. But, to begin, we must understand and be able to articulate the virtues of capitalism.

CHAPTER TWO

THE VIRTUES OF CAPITALISM

In 1969, Ezra Taft Benson wrote that, "[d]uring the last several years many of our institutions of learning have been turning out an increasing number of students schooled in amorality, relativity, and atheism—students divested of a belief in God, without fixed moral principles or an understanding of our constitutional republic and our capitalistic, free enterprise economic system" (Ezra Taft Benson, *An Enemy Hath Done This* (Salt Lake City: Parliament Publishers, 1969, 1994), 283). Today, fifty years later, the situation is much worse. Benson said that some have remarked that "the ninth wonder of the world is the apparent willingness of the American people to give up our free enterprise, capitalistic system because of a lack of appreciation and understanding of how the system works" (Benson, 256).

Capitalism is synonymous with freedom and prosperity. Ezra Taft Benson said, "the competitive price, free market, capitalistic system [is] the best system in this world" (Benson, 261). Conversely, socialism is synonymous with slavery, oppression, poverty and evil. When you understand both capitalism and socialism you will come to agree with these statements.

Capitalism is a key component of America's free enterprise system. Perhaps it would be better if our system of capitalism would be identified as the "free enterprise system," rather than capitalism because the word "free" is a powerful, positive label. But in this discussion, I intend to point out the many positive aspects of capitalism. I will not back away from the term. Rather I will confront the socialists and their false labels and false arguments that attack capitalism. Capitalism is not inherently negative any more than freedom is a negative. Just as freedom allows for people to make choices (good or bad), so does capitalism allow for both good choices and bad ones. Capitalism is not inherently bad. Rather, capitalism means that people have the freedom to invest their "capital" in projects and ventures of their own choosing. Capitalism stands for freedom, whereby people can create, invest, produce, manage and market ideas and turn them into prosperity. By focusing on the root meaning of capitalism, it becomes apparent that the term is really a good one.

The essence of capitalism is the individual ownership of "capital," or, in other words: private ownership of property. Capitalism doesn't exist where the government owns and controls all the property. And, by definition, that is what socialism is: the government owns and controls property. Capital is merely property that is available to be invested. Capital is inanimate—it is not a living thing—of itself it is neither good nor bad. But capital is more than just a thing—it is something of value that is owned by a person. Capital represents the essence of liberty—that is the right of a person to own and control property of value. A capitalist society is one that gives individuals the right to own and control their own property—unlike socialist and communist societies, where the government, not the individuals, owns and controls all the property. The freedom and right to control property is what gives individuals the incentive and opportunity to create, to make, to produce and to reap profits and rewards. Capitalism is the engine of economic prosperity. Socialism cannot provide this same incentive for its workforce. Socialism only motivates by threats and force and fear. But these motivations are not sufficient to energize and grow an entire economy, and history has borne this out.

Socialists say that government control of all property is good because they say the government can make sure everyone gets his/her fair share of property. But that is the problem with socialism—it is the government and not the individual who owns and controls property. In socialism the individual is not free to invest his/her property in projects and ventures that he/she believes will be profitable or worthy. In socialism, the government makes all those decisions. Therefore, socialism deprives itself of the diversity and creativity and personal incentives that are the foundation of prosperity in the free enterprise system. Without private ownership and control of property, there is no incentive, and there is no free enterprise.

Capitalism is the one word that best symbolizes both the freedom and the prosperity that has been achieved in the free enterprise economic system.

Historically, it is capitalism that is responsible for the major technological advances that have occurred in the last 150 years. These advances have made some men rich, but the benefits to society have been well worth it. Consider the following men and their work:

Henry Ford (the automobile)
Thomas Edison (light bulb, phonograph & harnessing electricity)
Andrew Carnegie (steel)
Alexander Graham Bell (telephone)
John D. Rockefeller (gas and oil)
Cornelius Vanderbilt (railroad)
William C. Durant (refrigeration)
Willis Carrier (air conditioning)

In more recent years, it is capitalism that has wrought even greater technological advances that have changed and blessed the world, and it has made some people wealthy along the way. But the world is better for it all. Consider these men and their accomplishments:

Bill Gates and Paul Allen (Microsoft)
Steve Jobs (Apple)
Jeff Bezos (Amazon)
Larry Page and Sergey Brin (Google)
Mark Zuckerberg (Facebook)

It is the freedom and opportunity afforded by capitalism that allows for these marvelous technological advances that have transformed the world.

Nevertheless, the socialists continue to insist that socialism is better than capitalism. The socialists continue to criticize and slam and smear capitalism; they call it evil, unfair and repressive. They label those who have capital as selfish, rich people who oppress the poor. But they are wrong. Sure, there are always some selfish rich, but that is the price of freedom. But capitalism has produced the most prosperity for more people in America and around the world than any other economic system.

It is more than a coincidence that the publication of Adam Smith's book, *The Wealth of Nations*, in 1776, coincided with the year that America declared its independence from Great Britain. Adam Smith is regarded as the father of the capitalism/free enterprise system. In his book, Adam Smith said this:

> The natural effort of every individual to better his own, condition, when suffered to exert itself with freedom and security, is so powerful a principle, that it is alone, and without any assistance, not only capable of carrying on the society to wealth and prosperity, but of surmounting a hundred impertinent obstructions with which the folly of human laws too often incumbers its operations; though the effect of these obstructions is always more or less either to encroach upon its freedom, or to diminish its security." (Benson, 140)

Abraham Lincoln said: "[I]t is best for all to leave each man free to acquire property as fast as he can. Some will get wealthy. I don't believe in a law to prevent a man from getting rich; it would do more harm than good. . . . I want every man to have the chance—and I believe a black man is entitled to it—in which he can better his position" (Benson, 234).

The esteemed American economist Milton Friedman, said this about capitalism: "There has never in history been a more effective machine for eliminating poverty than the free enterprise system and the free market. . . . If you look at the real problems of poverty and denial of freedom to people in this country, almost every single one of them are a result of government action and would be eliminated if you eliminated the bad government failures" (Milton Friedman, *Capitalism and Freedom* -- Stanford U. 1978).

Senator Strom Thurmond explained it this way:

> Capitalism, or the free enterprise system, is in essence economic liberty, and it goes hand in hand with political liberty. It rests on the basic idea of human rights in property, for where there are no human rights to own property, then there are no other human rights and freedoms. Take away a man's right to own property and you take away his right to be independent, substituting serfdom in place of freedom." (Benson, 20)

G. Edward Griffin explained that prosperity "is impossible without industrious and efficient production," and that that "is impossible without energetic, willing and eager labor," and that that "is not possible without incentive." Griffin continued, "[T]he freedom to attain a reward for one's labors is the most sustaining for most people. Sometimes called the profit motive, it is simply the right to plan and to earn and to enjoy the fruits of your labor." But Griffin then pointed out: "This profit motive diminishes as government controls, regulations and taxes increase to deny the fruits of success to those who produce. Therefore, any attempt *through governmental intervention* to redistribute the material rewards of labor can only result in the eventual destruction of the productive base of society, without which real abundance and security for more than the ruling elite is quite impossible."[4]

It is worthy to note that the right of the individual to own and control property is not a right that is mentioned in the Constitution. But this omission does not alter the fact that it is the most fundamental of all aspects of liberty and freedom. Without the right to own and control property there is no liberty. Socialists do not appreciate this. Some socialists deny that ownership of property is an important element of liberty. But they are wrong. They do not understand how ownership and control of one's property is the foundation of freedom and of a prosperous economy. Milton Friedman said that "[u]nderlying most arguments against the free market system is a lack of belief in freedom itself."[5] The socialists embrace Marx's plan of forced equality, which they falsely proclaim brings freedom. They are wrong. As Milton Friedman also said: "The society that puts equality before freedom will end up with neither. The society that puts freedom before equality will end up with a great measure of both" (*Id.*). Forced equality can bring a measure of equality to the amount of property people own. But it accomplishes this at the expense of freedom, and at the expense of creativity, initiative, and personal sacrifice to achieve. Socialism might bring more equality of property in the short run. But in the long run it is the agent of economic ruin for 99% of society, and the opportunity of enrichment is only for those few who control government.

Capitalism has been relentlessly criticized and condemned by the socialists and the communists. And while the criticism is false, the never-ending criticism has nevertheless been effective in building opposition to capitalism, such that for many people capitalism has come

---

[4] G. Edward Griffin, *The Fearful Master*, p. 128, quoted in Benson, 139.

[5] https://www.goodreads.com/author/quotes/5001.milton-friedman, accessed Sep. 4, 2019.

to have a negative connotation. This is an error that should be corrected, and I will attempt to do just that. Capitalism is the essential ingredient of freedom because only a free people can own and control property—i.e. own capital. When the government owns and controls all the property then there can be no private capital, therefore there can be no capitalism. The essence of capitalism is that the individual people control the property, and through their freedom and their choices they decide whether, when and how much capital to invest in business ventures. When government controls the property, the people do not have the freedom nor the ability to decide what businesses to support; neither do the people even have the right to decide where to work and where to live. When government controls all the property, the people have to do what the government directs. Even to the poor people this is a big deal because they may prefer to have the right to decide where to work and where to live, as well as the opportunity to become rich.

But, back to capitalism—the genius of its success is that it is founded on the principles of freedom: the freedom to choose where one works; the freedom to own and control private property; the freedom to invest that property in the business of one's choice; the freedom to start a business; the freedom to take a chance at an investment opportunity; the ability to fail, but the freedom to try again and again and again; the freedom and right to keep the profits of one's business when it succeeds.

In 1943, shortly after the U.S. entered into World War II, Apostle Stephen L. Richards made these comments about the virtues of capitalism, and the dangers of socialism:

> Many people misinterpret capitalism. They think that because the word capital is used to designate the system that its chief purpose is to make wealthy men who are usually called capitalists, and whose wealth it is feared is too often accumulated at the expense of the poorer classes. . . . But this is not the true concept of capitalism. In its inner essence it is little, if anything, more than a man's free right to work, to choose his work, and to enjoy the rewards of his efforts. In my estimation it is a most precious thing, and it is indispensable to the liberty and freedom of which America boasts. It is the only tried and tested system of free enterprise in this world and every other opposing system is built on an abridgement of personal liberty. We are fighting for it, and we are determined we will not lose it.
>
> But we will lose it some day if we do not understand it and

recognize its virtues. It is not the capitalistic system itself that makes some men rich and some men poor. The men themselves do that, again with some exceptions. The system merely offers the opportunities. . . . It does not guarantee that all men will be rich, and it is worthy of note that all systems which do, usually succeed only in making all poor. . . .

We must be patient with our American system. . . . I believe that the war effort [World War II], . . . has certainly indicated . . . a common desire to maintain our fundamental liberties, one of the most important of which is our system of free enterprise. (Stephen L. Richards, *The Church in War and Peace* (Salt Lake City: Deseret Book Co., 1943), 33-34)

These rights to own and control property are the foundation of individual freedom, and they are also the foundation of prosperity in America. No nation in the history of the world has achieved the widespread prosperity for more people than has America. And it is the freedom of capitalism that has made this happen.

Capitalism is responsible for the following improvements in the life of the average American worker from 1850 to 1958: (a) increasing the wages by 3 ½ times; (b) reducing the weekly hours of work from 70 to 40; and (c) increasing the number of jobs, bringing America closer to "full employment" than any other nation in the world (W. Cleon Skousen, *The Naked Communist* (Salt Lake City: The Ensign Publishing Co., 1958, 1962), 338). In addition, Skousen points out that capitalism is the best system for promoting technological advances, and it is the best system yet discovered by mankind for "sharing the wealth"—it permits everyone to make a profit, which can eliminate classes in society (Skousen, 342). Skousen explains that "[t]he genius of Capitalism is [that] . . . it responds to the factor of variation as between individuals. It allows each man to do anything he wishes so long as he can survive at it. . . . [Capitalism] allows a man to do just about whatever he wants to do. Laborers are not conscripted nor told they cannot strike; nor are they ordered to remain in certain occupations as tends to be the case in socialized and communized countries" (Skousen, 331). Capitalism creates jobs and prosperity for millions of people. Capitalism has done more to bring more people out of poverty than socialism ever did.

Unfortunately, the doctrines of socialism have been a mainstay in America's public schools for decades. Every year our public schools and most of the nation's universities graduate a new crop of socialists who are eager to change the world by bringing socialist philosophies and policies into our government and our laws. America's education system is infected with socialist propaganda which relentlessly disparages capitalism. Fortunately, there are enough informed people in America so that up until now some socialist proposals have been rejected. But socialist propaganda nevertheless takes a big toll on the students, more and more of whom are becoming socialists. The reason that socialism has not yet taken total control over all of America's laws and economy is because eventually many people come to recognize the lies and deceit of socialism. And then they begin to appreciate and support capitalism.

Capitalism does not require a lot of regulation or control by government. This is good because government regulation always increases the cost of goods and services. Government produces no products or services that the private sector cannot provide cheaper and better. Government produces red tape and increased administrative costs. The private sector can always be more efficient and profitable than government. Whatever government does, it does more expensively than the private sector. As Ezra Taft Benson pointed out: "A dollar cannot make the round trip to Washington and back without shrinking in the process" (Benson, 23).

Milton Friedman explained that "the preservation of freedom requires the elimination of . . . concentrated power to the fullest extent possible. . . . By removing the organization of economic activity from the control of political authority, the market eliminates this source of coercive power. It enables economic strength to be a check to political power" (Friedman, *Capitalism and Freedom,* p. 15, quoted in Jerreld L. Newquist, *Prophets, Principles and National Survival* (Salt Lake City: Publishers Press, 1964, 1976), 168).

Johan Norberg concludes that "economic freedom increases equality" (Johan Norberg, *In Defense of Global Capitalism* (Sweden: Timbro, 2001), 81). Norberg cited two Swedish studies that showed that those nations that introduced more freedom in their economies also experienced increased equality among their citizens.[6]

The creating of a big government to take care of the people was never the purpose of our Constitutional government. In fact, the Constitution specifically limited the powers of the federal government to prevent this type of encroachment into the lives of the people and the

---

[6] *Id.,* 81-82. The studies were done by G. W. Scully, 1992 and Niclas Berggren, 1999.

states. In his First Inaugural Address, in 1801, Thomas Jefferson said this about the proper role of government in relation to the prosperity of the people:

> With all these blessings, what more is necessary to make us a happy and prosperous people? Still one thing, fellow citizens—a wise and frugal government, which shall restrain men from injuring one another, which shall leave them otherwise free to regulate their own pursuits of industry and improvement, and shall not take from the mouth of labor the bread it has earned." (Benson, 139)

Ezra Taft Benson, who for eight years was Secretary of Agriculture in the Eisenhower Administration, had many opportunities to compare the effectiveness of socialist agricultural production with that in a free enterprise system. Benson said: "We must ever remember that a planned and subsidized economy weakens initiative, discourages industry, destroys character, and demoralizes the people" (Benson, 24). In America, with capitalism, "we really do have something better than anywhere else, and we shouldn't be ashamed to say so" (Benson, 233). **Capitalism is the one word that best symbolizes both the freedom and the prosperity that has been achieved in the free enterprise economic system.**

CHAPTER THREE

THE PROBLEMS OF SOCIALISM

The appeal of socialism is often enticing to the poor, but the benefits are short-termed at best, and there are virtually no long-term benefits. Socialism invariably crushes initiative and eventually impoverishes those who are subjected to it. You cannot find any socialist government that has ever brought its subjects to a state of prosperity. It has never worked. Socialism failed in the Soviet Union; it has failed in Cuba; it has failed in Venezuela. Socialism, the identical twin of communism has succeeded in impoverishing its subjects. It has succeeded in murdering those who oppose it.[7] It has succeeded in

---

[7] Let's not forget that in the course of establishing communism by force in Russia, Lenin murdered an estimated 100,000 to a million of his people. ("Red Terror," *Wikipedia*, Sep. 4, 2019.), Stalin murdered several million of his people. (Current scholarship attributes an estimated ten million deaths to Stalin, including 799,455 documented executions, 1.5 million deaths in the gulags, and about 6 million deaths caused by famines as to which Stalin refused assistance for those suffering in order to gain control over the people. "Joseph Stalin," *Wikipedia* Sep. 4, 2019.) And Khrushchev murdered million people. During the Stalin regime, Khrushchev was one of Stalin's most loyal and effective executioners, such that Khrushchev was personally responsible for millions of the deaths under Stalin's direction. The people of Ukraine placed the blame at Khrushchev's feet for as many as 400,000 deaths as a result of Stalin purges. (See "Crimes of Khrushchev against the Ukrainian People," *Wikipedia*, Sep. 4, 2019, citing www.ukrweekly.com > old > archives. The archived article is from *The Ukraine Weekly*, September 17, 1960, by Dr. Lev E. Dobriansky and several others.)

empowering dictators who control the entire government as it oppresses and enslaves the people. But it does not bring prosperity to all.

Ezra Taft Benson explained: "Communism [like socialism] is totalitarianism in which government control has been extended to practically every phase of human life" (Benson, 66-67). "The Soviet constitution reflects this philosophy in its emphasis on security: food, clothing, housing, medical care—the same things that might be considered in jail. The basic concept is that the government has full responsibility for the welfare of the people and, in order to discharge that responsibility, must assume control of all their activities. . . . [M]aterial gain and economic security simply cannot be guaranteed by any government. They are the result and reward of hard work and industrious production." (Benson, 138)

The fundamental flaw of socialism is that it undermines and impairs the economy by destroying the fundamental motivations to work and produce and make profit. Skousen explained: "The Communist leaders have suppressed the natural desires of their people and have tried to motivate them to action through fear. But this has not worked because fear is primarily a depressant instead of a stimulant. . . . "Work through fear" can never compete successfully with the tantalizing opportunity provided by Capitalism" which is the "power for Capitalism's productive momentum" (Skousen, 330).

The origin of modern-day socialism dates back to November, 1847, when Marx and Engels published their "Manifesto to the World" which, "announced to mankind that the new program of International Communism stood for: 1. The overthrow of capitalism, 2. The abolition of private property, 3. The elimination of the family as a social unit, 5. The abolition of all classes, 5. The overthrow of all governments, and 6. The establishment of a communist order with communal ownership of property in a classless, stateless society.[8]

---

[8] Skousen, 17-18. Skousen reports that Lenin wrote: "Marxism cannot be conceived without atheism." Lenin, "Religion," Introduction, pp. 3-6, quoted in Skousen, 330. Lenin also said: "A young man or woman cannot be a Communist youth unless he or she is free of religious convictions," quoted in Skousen, 307. The Russian Commissioner of Education, Lunarcharsky said this: "We hate Christians and Christianity. Even the best of them must be considered our worst enemies. Christian love is an obstacle to the development of the revolution." Quoted in the U. S. Congressional Record, Vol. 77, pp. 1539-1540, which was quoted in Skousen, 308.

For purposes of the discussion in this chapter, I will focus on the economic system of socialism, rather than on some other aspects that are often associated with socialism—that it is atheistic, dictatorial, anti-family, deceitful, and oppressive form of government. Communist leaders are quite content to stay in the background while America adopts socialist policies while it pretends that a socialist system can be adopted without also being atheist, anti-family, deceitful and oppressive of others. There is good reason to dispute this. (See chapter IV, below.) But for the moment, let us review merely the economic aspects of socialism. An examination of them makes it clear that the socialist economic system is a flawed, oppressive, discouraging, and impoverishing system, such that it brings poverty and enslavement and misery wherever it is fully implemented.

Former FBI Director Dan Smoot said this in 1968: "The economic and social cannibalism produced by this communist-socialist idea will destroy any society which adopts it and clings to it as a basic principle—any society"(Benson, 140). Henry Grady Weaver explained it this way, in his book *The Mainspring of Human Progress*:

> Most of the major ills of the world have been caused by well-meaning people who ignored the principle of individual freedom, except as applied to themselves, and who were obsessed with fanatical zeal to improve the lot of mankind-in-the-mass through some pet formula of their own. . . . *The harm done by ordinary criminals, murderers, gangsters, and thieves is negligible in comparison with the agony inflicted upon human beings by the professional "do-gooders,"* who attempt to set themselves up as gods on earth and would ruthlessly force their views on all others—with the abiding assurance that the end justifies the means." (Weaver, pp. 40-41, quoted in Benson, 140)

Milton Friedman concurs. He said that if we are to preserve our freedom we must beware of "the internal threat coming from men of good intentions and good will who wish to reform us. Impatient with the slowness of persuasion . . . to achieve the great social changes they envision, they are anxious to use the power of the state to achieve their ends" (Friedman, *Capitalism and Freedom*, 201, quoted in Newquist, 317). Friedman said that "[f]reedom is a rare and delicate plant," and that we must be on the guard to "keep the government we create from becoming a Frankenstein that will destroy the very freedom we establish it to protect" (*Id.*, 340).

Another of the basic flaws in socialism is the "class warfare" that it encourages "between 'capitalists' and working men, between management and labor. Communist [and socialist] agitators preach class hatred between these two groups and attempt to mobilize the workers into a class war against their employers" (Benson, 234). Continuing, Benson said: "[M]anagement and labor are not class enemies, but are equal partners in the mutual business enterprise of producing the goods and services that make our high standard of living possible. Neither can exist without the other. Likewise, neither can be hurt without the other eventually being hurt. If management's wages (called profits) are squeezed to where management either raises the price of its product or goes out of business, then labor either pays a higher price for the product in the store or is out of a job. . . . . The relationship between employer and employee is based upon the natural laws of supply and demand" (Benson, 234-235).

Another flaw with socialism is its appeal to the masses to get something for nothing. Theodore Roosevelt said: "The things that will destroy America are prosperity-at-any-price, peace-at-any-price, safety-first instead of duty-first, the love of soft living and the get-rich-quick theory of life." (Ezra Taft Benson, *The Red Carpet*, p. 315.) This is repulsive to every God-fearing person.

Even if one were inclined to be tolerant of the views of socialists, it is important to recognize that socialists are not tolerant of capitalists—socialists seek to destroy capitalism. Socialists invariably seem to take the same position as the twentieth century socialist who said: "We are socialists, we are enemies of today's capitalistic economic system . . . . and we are all determined to destroy this system under all conditions."[9] The man who said this was Gregor Strasser, a one-time associate of Adolf Hitler. In World War II, Nazi Germany was just as much a socialist nation as the Soviet Union. "Hitler was an excellent disciple of Lenin and Stalin, a perfect product of totalitarianism. The heinous Nazi crimes were the outcome of a consistent application of totalitarian

---

[9] This quote is often attributed to Adolf Hitler, and Hitler may have used it on occasion. But the quote originated from Gregor Strasser, *Thoughts about the Tasks of the Future* (1926). Hitler and Strasser worked together in the formative years of the Nazi Party. But the two eventually developed strong differences, and in 1934 Hitler had him assassinated during the Rohm purge. See https:www//snopes.com/fact-check/hitler-nazis-capitalist-system/ checked on September 9, 2019.

principles" (Benson, *An Enemy*, 67). The Soviet Union and Nazi Germany were both totalitarian governments.

All governments work by force, whether they are dictatorships or democracies. The difference is that the dictator unilaterally makes all the government decisions, while in democracies the people vote to empower the government to do things. Nevertheless, governments always act with force to do things. George Washington said: "Government is not reason, it is not eloquence—it is force! Like fire, it is a dangerous servant and a fearful master!" (Benson, *An Enemy*, 24). But while all governments work by force, democratic governments and limited governments are best because they have a tendency to allow and protect the most freedoms of their people. Socialist and communist governments always tend to be repressive because they control more aspects of the lives of their citizens. This is not a matter of debate. Socialist governments restrict liberties more than free market capitalist governments. There is no question that there is more freedom in capitalism than in socialism. Historically, capitalism out-performs socialism every time in terms of both freedom and prosperity.

Judge Jeanine Pirro points out that "all socialism is eventually authoritarian" (Pirro, 228). She explains: "Socialism can't be maintained without authoritarianism because it defies human nature. It is in everyone's nature to pursue his or her individual economic interests, to pursue his or her own dreams. This is so basic a right it's in our Declaration of Independence. The pursuit of happiness is an individual right, not a collective one, and our Founding Fathers believe it is inalienable" (*Id.*, 228-229).

The essence of socialism is that government controls the nation's property so that it, the government, can redistribute it in a way that is "fair." But what does "fair" mean? Socialists promise to take property from the wealthy and distribute it to those with less to bring about an equality of property holdings among all the people. This system has never succeeded in improving the level of living of its people. Socialism has always failed. It is easy to see why: **First**, Socialism removes "incentive, creativity and diligence from its workers. Socialism removes from its economy the positive motivation to bring innovation and increased productivity. **Second**, and totally inter-connected with the first, in socialism the government owns and controls all of the property. **Third**, and also inter-connected with the first two—the citizens under socialism are deprived of the most fundamental freedoms. The person who cannot improve his wealth by acquiring property, has no freedom to choose the business or profession of his/her choice. Under socialism the worker does not control where and when and for whom he works. Some proponents of socialism today insist that people cannot be forced to do work that they do not want to do. (Actually, I don't believe this is true. When a socialist government dispenses income, food, housing, medical care and other benefits to its people, the government invariably requires the recipients to do what they are told. This is how the totalitarian socialist governments maintain control over their people.) **Fourth**, and also inter-connected with the first three is the slavery to which all citizens submit. In socialism, the citizens bargain to get security, and they give up their liberty in exchange for it. The crazy part of this is that socialism never delivers what it promises—it never delivers the better life style that it promises, and the enslavement continues even after the system has been proven a fraud.

Another problem with socialism is the impossibility to make a fair "re-distribution" of wealth. The re-distribution can never possibly be perfectly fair because it cannot possibly deal with the many differences in the needs and wants and desires of the people. The ideal in socialism is to make sure that all people have fair and equal amounts of food, housing, health care, vacation, and retirement. But this aspirational goal is never achievable. Ultimately, the redistribution is always "somebody's" opinion and judgment about what is best—there will always be some "person" whose judgment and power is in charge—this becomes a de facto dictatorship. While many people may be deceived into thinking that "government knows best," the fact remains that the redistribution will always reflect the views of whatever individuals are in power at the time. Thus, by definition socialism always becomes a totalitarian dictatorship controlled by somebody. Socialism is the opposite of a free economic system where the individual can decide how he/she wants to make a living, where the individual can take economic risks and then keep the rewards of his/her work, and then has the freedom to change professions any time. These fundamental freedoms are not a part of socialism.

Another inherent problem with socialism is to determine what will be the income level or standard of living of its people. To be specific with one aspect of socialism, health care: What will be the level or quality of health care that all will get? The issue surfaces in a thousand different ways: Will the patient have his/her own room, or will it be a shared room? Will the patient be entitled to the best surgeon in the world, or just whoever is on call at the local hospital? Will the patient have the right to go to the best hospital in the region, or must he/she accept whatever level of service is available locally? Is a particular medical procedure necessary? And is the procedure "covered" by government health care? If not, the individual can't have the procedure, whether or not he wants it. By definition, in socialism each person should get the same level of care. But it will never happen. Further, it is inevitable that either (a) the people will constantly complain that it is too low, or (b) if the system provides a more expensive level of care than it can afford, this will drive the system into bankruptcy. Furthermore, (c) there will never be a fair and equal sharing of property because there are too many differences in peoples' conditions, desires and needs. Dissatisfaction with the level of health care is a constant in socialism.

The attack socialism makes on freedom is sometimes lost on some people because socialism focuses on helping the poor, which in and of itself can be a good thing. But the methods of socialism are evil; socialism promises to share the wealth of the rich to make everyone equal in food, clothing, housing, health care and property. But the methods of socialism take away freedom from the rich and the poor. Socialism takes away private ownership and control of property, and puts property in the control of the government which redistributes it in the way it feels is best.

Superficially, socialism can sound appealing—as a way to help the poor. But socialism is not the only way to help the poor, and it is not the best way. The best way is through capitalism. First, capitalism is the best economic system to create jobs for the most people. Second, capitalism gives people the opportunity to help others (which they would not have in socialism); through the charity and compassion of those who are able, capitalism enables the good people to assist those in need. Government assistance for the poor is best accomplished on the state, local and individual levels—rather than from the federal government.

Since socialism is philosophically flawed, it is no wonder that historically it has never brought prosperity to those who practiced it. Socialism has never produced the prosperity it promises. Socialism has always worsened the economies of the nations that have embraced it. Thus, those who propose socialism are ignorant of the lessons of history as well as being dupes of a philosophically-flawed economic system.

Currently in America, private ownership of property continues to be allowed, but it is subject to substantial taxes (including income taxes) that take as much as 50% or more of citizens' income. At some point, as taxes get high, it effectively reduces the individual right to own property. When taxes get too high, this "weaken[s] the incentives of the wealthy to risk in new business ventures with money they already have. Why should they? If the venture should fail, they absorb the loss. But if it should succeed, they have to pay most of the profits in taxes. In a sense, they are penalized for success. It is much easier to sit back, avoid the extra work, live comfortably, and not take the risk" (Benson, *An Enemy*, 224). Thus, excessive income taxes weaken incentive, slow the expansion of businesses, and reduce the number of new jobs created. (*Id.*)

Ezra Taft Benson concluded with this:

> It is high time we awakened to the dangers of excessive government in business, in education, in agriculture, and other segments of our economy. It is time we realized the perils of too great a centralization of power, and too much dependence on public agencies. We must stand up and be counted. I agree with Tom Anderson: " . . . Why change the American system which produced the greatest freedom for the greatest number of people in human history, along with the world's highest standard of living, for socialism." (Benson, *An Enemy*, 19)

There are a couple of amazing things about the socialists' resiliency in claiming how beneficial socialism is. First, despite the fact that it has never lived up to its promises, its adherents nevertheless are unabashedly certain that it will usher in utopia now. Second, it is remarkable to see how America's educators vouch for the benefits of socialism without any historical basis to support its promises. For whatever reason, educators have embraced socialism as the ideal form of government, but without good reasons to support their conclusions. America's education system has been co-opted by the communists and socialists, who insist that the purpose of government is to make people do good. Socialists assert that the people, of themselves, will not do good, and that the government must tell them what to do. This approach denies the goodness of mankind, and attempts to enforce one person's brand of goodness on everyone else.

America's educators have swallowed the deceptive propaganda of the communists hook, line and sinker. This exposes the educators to be either uninformed or lazy or victims to the peer pressure of their fellow teachers. Whatever the reason, the result is still disgraceful: American educators do a great disservice to the nation and to our youth. And worse than that, American educators are hurting our nation; they are causing strife and discontent and an entitlement mentality, and they are contributing to an eroding of our liberties and of individual and national prosperity.

Socialism was exposed, understood and condemned by the world's greatest leaders in the past, but today's rising generation doesn't seem to be aware of this. That is because their educators have withheld this information from them. As far as civics and history go, much of today's education system is more indoctrination than education. Did you know that in World War II America was fighting against the Nazis *and their socialism*? Let me now supply some of the statements of great leaders in the twentieth century, and show what they had to say about socialism.

Winston Churchill made the following statements about socialism: "Socialism is the philosophy of failure, the creed of ignorance, and the gospel of envy. Its inherent virtue is the equal sharing of misery." "No Socialist Government conducting the entire life and industry of the country could afford to allow free, sharp, or violently-worded expressions of public discontent. They would have to fall back on some form of Gestapo." "Socialism is an attack on the right to breathe freely. No socialist system can be established without a political police."

President Ronald Reagan said this about socialism: "A socialist is someone who has read Lenin and Marx. An anti-socialist is someone who understands Lenin and Marx."

Margaret Thatcher said this: "The problem with socialism is that you eventually run out of other peoples' money." "Good conservatives always pay their bills. Unlike socialists, who just run up other people's bills." And, as far as paying bills in concerned, Ezra Taft Benson pointed out: "A government which is unable to pay its own bills can hardly be depended upon to pay yours" (Benson, *An Enemy*, 220). As demonstrated in the collapse of the Soviet Union in 1989, socialism leads to financial ruin, not prosperity.

The French historian Alexis de Tocqueville said this: "Democracy and socialism have nothing in common but one word, equality. But notice the difference: while democracy seeks equality in liberty, socialism seeks equality in restraint and servitude."

According to former FBI Director J. Edgar Hoover: " A tragedy of the past generation in the United States is that so many persons, including high- ranking statesmen, public officials, educators, ministers of the Gospel, professional men, have been duped into helping communism. . . . We cannot defeat Communism with Socialism, nor with secularism . . . . We can only defeat Communism with true Americanism."[10]

And what did Hoover mean by "Americanism"? He meant what was described by Dean Alfange:

> I do not choose to be a common man. It is my right to be uncommon. I seek opportunity to develop whatever talents God gave me – not security. I do not wish to be a kept citizen, humbled and dulled by having the state look after me. I want to take the calculated risk; to dream and to build, to fail and to succeed. I refuse to barter incentive for a dole. I prefer the challenges of life to the guaranteed existence; the thrill of fulfillment to the stale calm of utopia. I will not trade freedom for beneficence nor my dignity for a handout. . . . All this is what it means to be an American.[11]

Ezra Taft Benson said: "Ours is an era when socialism and social justice are confused; liberty is confused with license; morality is confused with pleasure; and constitutionality is confused with practicality. . . . College campuses under the bountiful federal government have become centers of radicalism; teach-ins, lecture-ins, sit-ins, demonstrations, 'communist fronts'. . . " (Benson, *An Enemy*, 101). Benson continued: "There is no freedom under full socialism. Our fight is freedom vs. creeping socialism. Socialism is simply: Government ownership and control of the means of production and distribution" (Benson, *An Enemy*, 255).

Marion G. Romney gave this advice: "We must be careful that we are not led to accept or support in any way any organization, cause or measure which in its remotest effort, would jeopardize free agency, whether it be in politics, government, religion, employment, education, or in any other field. It is not enough for us to be sincere in what we support. We must be right!" (Benson, *An Enemy*, 291)

---

[10] Address by J. Edgar Hoover, Oct. 9, 1962, quoted in Newquist, 288.

[11] Statement by Dean Alfange, quoted in Benson, *An Enemy*, 11.

"Finally, when the going gets rough, we mustn't rush to Washington and ask Big Brother to take care of us through price controls, rent controls, guaranteed jobs and wages. Any government powerful enough to give the people all that they want is also powerful enough to take from the people all that they have" (Benson, *An Enemy,* 220-221).

CHAPTER FOUR

THE EVIL OF SOCIALISM

To say that socialism is bad is one thing, but to call it "evil" is something else. Nevertheless, for the reasons that will be given in this chapter, I will show why socialism is evil. In doing this I am not engaging in an exercise of name-calling; that is not my purpose. But my purpose is to make it clear that socialism—even if it could be distinguished from atheistic communism—is a very bad and destructive economic system; socialism is so bad that it is evil. Socialism is not just a less desirable economic system than capitalism. Socialism is evil, masquerading as virtue. It is a fraud that needs to be exposed.

Although Karl Marx' parents were devout Christians, Marx rejected both Christianity and a belief in God.[12] Marx was openly atheistic in the communism that he advocated. Marx denied that there was a God and that there was a divine purpose in life; Marx said that his purpose was "to dethrone God and destroy capitalism" (Skousen, 37). Lenin later reinforced this: "Marxism cannot be conceived without atheism."[13] Lenin said that communists "must combat religion."[14] On another occasion Lenin said: "A young man or woman cannot be a Communist youth unless he or she is free of religious convictions."[15] As

---

[12] Marx repudiated all forms of Religion. He claimed the four Gospels were forgeries, that Jesus was a figure of fiction, and that Christianity was a fraud. Skousen, 12.

[13] V. I. Lenin, "Religion," Introduction, pp. 3-6, quoted in Skousen, 310.

[14] V. I. Lenin, "Religion," pp. 14 & 349, quoted in Skousen, 307.

[15] Lenin, "Young Communist Truth," October 18, 1947, quoted in Skousen, 307.

Lunarcharsky, the Russian Commissioner of Education, said: "We hate Christians and Christianity."[16]

Communism is specifically rooted in denying the existence of God and repudiating all religion. And socialism is virtually identical to communism except that it often masquerades as being indifferent as to matters of religion. Thus, in modern America there are some socialists who claim to believe in God. For them, socialism is unrelated to religion; for them socialism is just an economic system. But the atheistic and anti-family and anti-freedom elements of communism are often present, such that they often manifest in the socialists' words and proposals. This is certainly the case with the 2019 versions of socialism advocated by some of the 2019 Democrat presidential contenders. Although America's modern socialists would deny that they are communists, their words belie this; their socialism still has some of the same major evil elements that are in pure communism.

Ezra Taft Benson explained that "[t]he socialist-communist philosophy is devastatingly evil—destructive of all that is good, uplifting and beautiful. It strikes at the very foundation of all we hold dear. The communist 'has convinced himself that nothing is evil which answers the call of expediency.' This is a most damnable doctrine. People who truly accept such a philosophy have neither conscience nor honor. Force, trickery, lies, broken promises—to them such things are wholly justified" (Benson, *An Enemy*, 91).

Beginning with Marx, and continuing with Lenin, Stalin, Khrushchev, and continuing today, there is no morality with communism. For communists, the end justifies the means. As openly acknowledged in an official statement on Radio Moscow on August 20, 1950: "[F]rom the point of view of Communist morality, only those acts are moral which contribute to the building up of a new Communist society" (Skousen, 305). It is my observation that the same is true today with socialists, who assert that their socialism is morally better than capitalism and that those who disagree are immoral and bad.

But socialism is also evil because it is inextricably connected to other evil components of communism—it prohibits free speech and individual rights; and it rules the people with totalitarian force.

---

[16] Lunarcharsky, quoted in the U. S. Congressional Record, Vol. 77, pp. 1539-1540, quoted in Skousen, 308.

Socialism is evil because it is an economic system that destroys both freedom and prosperity. Let me break this down and emphasize each part of this sentence. By definition socialism destroys freedom because **by force** it takes away property from some, **by force** it redistributes that property to others, **by force** it makes the recipients do what they're told, and **by force** it punishes (and sometimes kills) those who resist. Freedom is replaced by government control over who has what property. But socialism also destroys prosperity. Socialism undermines and eventually destroys prosperity because it eliminates the incentives and motivations to be productive. Without the ability to keep the fruits of one's hard work, prosperity is always impaired. And this is why socialism is impoverishing. The socialists' claim that socialism brings prosperity and freedom. But this is a lie. In addition, socialism uses force and oppression to reach its goals.

According to Marx, the economic components of socialism and communism are: "1. The overthrow of capitalism, 2. The abolition of private property, 3. The elimination of the family as a social unit, 5. The abolition of all classes, 5. The overthrow of all governments, and 6. The establishment of a communist order with communal ownership of property in a classless, stateless society."[17]

Not only are communism and socialism fatally flawed as an economic avenue to prosperity, but the means for its proponents to make socialism popular are evil. Socialism preaches hatred for those who oppose it. In 1946, Joseph Stalin stated: "It is impossible to conquer an enemy without having learned to hate him with all the might of one's soul."[18] An official Soviet Union statement in 1947 declared: "Hatred fosters vigilance and an uncompromising attitude toward the enemy.[19] This describes exactly what the socialists are doing to capitalists in 2019— they hate them and they demand that others also show their hatred for capitalists. Examples of this includes the liberal boycott against Chick-fil-A (who was targeted for its defending traditional Christian values), and it includes Hollywood's blacklisting of Trump supporters (that was reported on September 3, 2019).

---

[17] Skousen, 17-18, describing the Communist Manifesto, issued by Marx and Engels in November, 1847.

[18] Joseph Stalin, "The Great Patriotic War of the Soviet Union," Moscow, 1946, p. 55., quoted in Skousen, 308.

[19] Official Statement, quoted from the "SMALL SOVIET ENCYCLOPEDIA," Moscow, 1947, Vol XI, p. 1045, quoted in Skousen, 308.

Today's proponents of socialism attempt to differentiate socialism from communism. Insofar as socialism does not overtly deny God, then that is better than communism's overt fighting against God. But the essence of the socialistic philosophy is nevertheless evil because it denies its participants the freedom to control their property and their lives.

Socialism's guarantees of security and prosperity are a fraud. Socialism cannot provide what it promises. Initially it can take from the rich and spread it among the poor. But this short-term benefit to the poor ends when the wealth of the rich is used up. Then society reaps an equality of poverty. As Churchill said: "Its inherent virtue is the equal sharing of misery." Socialism is nothing more than a cheap, get-rich-quick scheme. It is superficially appealing to those who are uninformed and deceived. But being based upon principles of force and failure and dependence, socialism is at best a subterfuge. In fact, socialism is much worse—it is evil because it destroys freedom, restricts choices, and blocks the pursuit of happiness.

Let's get right to the heart of it. The problem with socialism is that it is an economic fraud. It promises equality of prosperity for all, but it delivers only equality of depression. It promises to raise the level of living of the poor by taking away the property of the rich. But it seeks to accomplish this by force—it takes away the property of those who have the ability to create and produce and innovate. In so doing, socialism eliminates the genius and the foundation of a profitable economy. In the short-term socialism can improve the standard of living of the poor, but this is soon dissipated when the property of the rich is depleted. This hobbles and undermines a prosperous economy. That is why socialism is a fraud—it promises prosperity, but its methods destroy initiative, productivity, and prosperity.

Judge Jeanine Pirro explained it this way:

> A socialist system can get along all right temporarily, depending upon how rich the country was before it was instituted. The people don't notice their rights being infringed because there is lots of free stuff being handed out. But as soon as the country's wealth is depleted, and the capitalist means aren't there to produce new wealth, the authoritarianism becomes necessary to prevent people from doing what they naturally do in tough circumstances—work had and attempt to keep the fruits of their own labor. (Pirro, 229)

Socialists are like sleezy shysters who offer the greedy masses "something for nothing." Socialists take advantage of the overly eager and gullible poor folks, selling them some "too-good-to-be-true" snake oil at a "once-in-a-lifetime" low price. Socialism is a sham and a scam. Those who embrace it give up their liberty to join. But once they have been taken in, they don't get prosperity—they only get the shaft. Then they're stuck, and they can't get out.[20]

The historic proponents of socialism were frauds, deceitful propagandists, revolutionaries, and evil manipulators. I'm talking about Marx, Engels, Lenin, Stalin, Khrushchev, Castro and leaders like them. These socialists openly deny the existence of God; they repudiate Christianity and traditional morality; they attack and denigrate the family; their moral standard is that whatever attacks capitalism and promotes socialism is good, and whatever promotes God, morality, family and capitalism is bad. Socialism turns upside-down the morality of freedom, calling good evil and evil good.

---

[20] This age-old shyster technique was described in more formal terms in 1942 by Heber J. Grant, J. Reuben Clark and David O. McKay, who said that the communists/socialists were "using a technique that is as old as the human race—a fervid, but false solicitude for the unfortunate, over whom they thus gain mastery, and then enslave them" (Statement of the First Presidency, quoted in Benson, *An Enemy*, 191).

CHAPTER FIVE

HISTORY OF SOCIALISM IN THE WORLD

The socialist propagandists are relentless. They will not acknowledge the flaws of socialism. Socialists advance their objectives by power and raw force. For socialists, truth and morality are only important when convenient.[21] Revolution, riots, chaos, dissent, protests, conflict, fighting and wars are all desirable for socialists—they help present opportunities to effect change through force.[22] If you don't believe this, you should review the history of how socialism and communism have come to be implemented in nations around the world. Russia's embrace of communism in 1917 came about this way. The spread of communism at the beginning of World War II was brought about in part because there was widespread fear of Nazi socialism. Today it is not often acknowledged that Stalin's communism and Hitler's socialism were almost identical.; but they were. Benson wrote: "[A]s Stalin watched Hitler cudgel and jostle his way into power he recognized in the Nazi dictator a formidable opponent of his own breed and kind. He saw that Hitler was shrewd and ruthless. He was completely amoral. He had no compunction whatever against violence, the purging of his own people, the use of deceit in propaganda, nor the sacrifice of millions of

---

[21] "Riots—demonstrations—street battles—detachments of a revolutionary army—such are the stages in the development of the popular uprising." V. I. Lenin, "SELECTED WORKS," Vol. III, p. 312, quoted in Skousen, 298.

[22] Abraham Lincoln said: "There is no grievance that is a fit object of redress by mob law" Benson, *An Enemy*, 189).

lives to achieve personal power. Materialism had produced precisely the same product in Germany that it had produced in Russia. Although called by different names Nazism and Communism were aimed at the same identical mark and were forged in very similar ideological molds." (Benson, *An Enemy*, 157)

Then, after World War II, Stalin used the instability of post-war Europe to expand communism. When America and Britain were weary of war, Stalin was able to help the communist leader Mao Tse-tung turn China communist and to defeat the freedom-loving patriot Chiang Kai-shek. The same happened in Korea and Vietnam. And American leadership allowed communism to take over half of both of those nations. Thousands of American soldiers lost their lives fighting those two wars, which the leaders never intended to win.[23] The same thing happened in Cuba in the 1950s—America stood by as Castro used the turmoil and unrest in Cuba to seize power and establish communism on an island 90 miles from Florida.

There has been an extensive spread of communism and socialism around the world in the last one hundred years. This growth is a threat to freedom and prosperity for all the world. In 1969, Ezra Taft Benson said that "[n]ever in recorded history has any movement spread itself so far and so fast as has socialistic-communism in the past few years. In less than half a century this evil system has gained control over one-third of mankind, and it is steadily pursuing its vicious goal of control over all the rest of the world. Since World War II, people have been brought under the communist yoke at the rate of . . . 52,000,000 per year" (Benson, *An Enemy*, 16). Fifty years later, the spread of socialism is even greater.

It is helpful to review the chart on the next pages to appreciate the growth of socialism during the last 150 years. Reading this chart will give an important summary of how socialism has grown to be a major force in the world today.

---

[23] "Secretary Robert McNamara asserted in October, 1966, that our objectives in Vietnam are limited, and do not include the destruction of the communist regime in North Vietnam" (Benson, *An Enemy*, 70). "The U.S. has suffered more than 60,000 casualties in this undeclared no-win war" (*Id.*, 84).

History of the Spread of Socialism in the World

1847	Marx and Engels publish *Manifesto*
1848	Marx fails to establish communism in the French Revolution
1849	Marx fails to establish communism in the German Revolution
1859	Charles Darwin publishes *On the Origin of Species*
1867	Marx publishes *Capital* (for violent overthrow of gov't)
1905	Lenin unsuccessful in attempt to take control of Russia
1917	Overthrow of Russia's Tsar's government; Lenin establishes communist rule under his leadership.[24]
1922	Mussolini (founder of fascism) becomes dictator in Italy
1923	Failed coup by Hitler in Munich. He is imprisoned one year.
1927	Mao Zedung (Tset-ung) founds communist party in China
1932	Hitler leads group that objects to the Treaty of Versailles (that ended World War I).
1933	Adolf Hitler appointed Chancellor of Germany. He quickly makes himself dictator.
1939	Germany invades Poland
1940	Germany invades Denmark, Norway, Finland, Estonia, Latvia, Lithuania, France, Luxemburg, Belgium & Netherlands
1940	Sept. 27th: Tripartite Pact signed—Germany, Italy & Japan form "Axis" powers to conquer the world. Later, Hungary, Romania, and Bulgaria joined the Axis.
1941	Germany invaded Yugoslavia & Greece; then Soviet Union
1941	Japan attacked the U.S. on December 7th
1941-45	WWII -- Soviet Union sided with GB and USA—the Allies
1943	Mussolini defeated in Italy—Allies take control of Italy
1944	D Day invasion on June 6th
1945	In April Mussolini is executed and Hitler commits suicide
1945	Germany surrenders in May; Japan surrenders in August
1945	Soviet Union consumes eastern Europe (Albania, Hungary, Yugoslavia, Romania, Bulgaria)
1945	After Japan surrendered, communists took over North Korea
1946	Soviet Union takes control of Bulgaria
1947	Soviet Union takes control of Poland
1948	Soviet Union seizes power in Czechoslovakia
1949	Soviet Union seizes control of E. Germany

---

[24] After the Tsar was overthrown, in an early election, 75% of the people voted against Lenin. Despite this, in the tumult of the revolution, Lenin used the power that he did have to imprison his opponents and to take control of the country (Skousen, 115).

1949	Mao Tse-tung drive Chiang Kai Chek (and Nationalists) from mainland China and on to Island of Taiwan. Mae Tse-tung established a communist government on mainland China.
1950	North Korea invades South Korea (Korean War 1950-53)
1954	most of Indochina taken over by Communists
1954	Vietnam independence from France—becomes communist in north, & democratic in south—Vietnam war (1955-73)
1959	Cuban dictator Batista was overthrown, and Fidel Castro took over, making it the first communist nation in Latin America
1973	America tired of Vietnam war, allows communists to take control of all of Vietnam
1975	Vietnam, Cambodia and Laos fall to communist control following victory by communists
1970s	Sandanista family in power in Nicaragua (communist ties)
1980s	US backs contras in Nicaragua
1989	Widespread financial ruin overtakes communist countries— Soviet Union falls apart[25]
1991	Kuwait War
1997	Hugo Chavez takes power in Venezuela (communist)
2001	Sept. 11 - Terrorist attacks in New York City & at Pentagon
2002	Iraq War starts (expands to Afghanistan)
2019	Venezuela nation in financial ruin—civil war

---

[25] This led to the formal dissolution of the Soviet Union in 1991. Thereafter, many of the states that had been a part of the Soviet Union, plus many of the other communist countries began to develop closer ties with Western Europe and the United States.

The fifteen states that became separate and sovereign with the dissolution of the Soviet Union are: Armenia, Azerbajan, Belarus, Estonia, Georgia, Kazakhstan, Krygzstan, Latvia, Lithuania, Moldova, Russia, Tajikistan, Turkmenistan, Ukraine and Uzbekistan.

Other nations that had been under communist control during the cold war began to reject communism and develop closer ties with the United States. Those nations include: Romania (joined NATO in 2004), Hungary (became a democratic republic in 1989), Poland (became a presidential democratic republic in 1989), East Germany (merged with Germany in 1990, repudiating communism and forming a more democratic government), and Austria (was liberated by the Allied Forces at the end of WW II, and it has remained independent of Russia). In 1989 Czechoslovakia rejected communism and re-established a democratic government, In 1989, Bulgaria rejected communist control and re-established a democratic government. Colossal financial failures in 1989 led to the rejection of communism as well as the break-up of Yugoslavia—eventually Croatia and Slovakia emerged as the two principal nations, which established democratic governments in 1992.

CHAPTER SIX

HISTORY OF SOCIALISM
IN AMERICA

The growth and expansion of socialism within the United States during the last century has also been extensive, and it represents a real threat to our future freedom and prosperity. The chart on the next page shows the dates of the main events in connection with the growth of socialism in America from 1913 to 2019. Reading this chart will give an important summary of the growth of socialism in America.

A. Initial Movements towards Socialism

America is not totally socialist, yet. But it has been gradually become more and more socialistic for a hundred years now. It started with passage of the income tax amendment (Amendment 16) in 1913. This enabled Congress to take virtually everything from the people by taxing income. This set the stage for socialism to be put in place, and that is exactly what happened beginning with the election of Franklin D. Roosevelt, following the stock market crash of 1929. After the election of Roosevelt in 1832, he proceeded to concoct multiple socialist programs for the nation. Congress rubber stamped virtually every proposal he made. Roosevelt transformed the American government long before Barack Obama promised to "transform" America. What Roosevelt did is acknowledged today to have wrought a gigantic adoption of socialism

History of the Growth of Socialism in America (1913-2019)

1913	16th Amendment is ratified, establishing a federal income tax
1933	U. S. recognizes the nation of Russia

Era of Initial Transformation from Capitalism towards Socialism

1933-39	Programs established in response to the Great Depression—significant socialist expansion in the federal government
1933	Prohibition repealed (Amendment 21)
1939	Germany conquers Austria, Poland & France
1941-45	U. S. in World War II
1945	Soviet Union takes control of Poland, Romania, Czechoslovakia, E. Germany & Hungary
1950-53	Korean War
1950s	Sen. Joseph McCarthy accuses many of being a communist
1954	Senate censures McCarthy
1961	Cuban Missile Crisis/Bay of Pigs
1963	JFK assassinated by a Soviet
1964	Barry Goldwater—press slam as extremist and imbalanced

Era of Creeping Socialism

1964-68	Lyndon Johnson's Great Society--War on Poverty, Housing, Food Stamps, Medicaid & Medicare, and Civil Rights
1969	Moon Landing
1970	Environmental Protection Agency (EPA) established
1972	Clean Water Act, Endangered Species Act
1973	Nixon pulls US out of Vietnam
1974	Nixon resigns
1980	Ronald Reagan elected President
1989	Fall of the Iron Curtain - Disintegration of the Soviet Union Nations freed: Eastern Europe, Hungary, Romania, Slovakia, Serbia, Poland, Ukraine
1989	Rush Limbaugh begins national radio programs
1991	Kuwait War
1992	Ross Perot factor—Bill Clinton elected President
1995	Welfare Reform—some control for welfare returned to States
1996	FOX News Network launched
1998	Clinton impeached
2001	Sept. 11 attacks
2002	Iraq War starts (expands to Afghanistan)

Era of Overt Socialism

2008	Election of Barack Hussein Obama
2009	Obama begins removing U. S. missiles from eastern Europe
2010	Affordable Care Act passed
2014	Russia takes over the Ukraine and Crimea
2016	Election of Donald Trump
2016-19	Fake news; Trump investigated for alleged conspiracy with Russia
2019	Mueller Report: No evidence Trump colluded with Russia

in America, and today many people praise Roosevelt for doing so.[26] But not everyone.

Roosevelt's programs were so radical that the long-time Democrat leader Alfred Smith (Democrat Presidential Nominee in 1928), made a major speech in 1936 in Washington, D.C. to his fellow Democrats, warning them that Roosevelt and the Democrat Party had abandoned their principles and had embraced socialism. Smith called on his party to cease their socialist programs and return to their traditional, core values that embraced freedom and the free enterprise system. I will include below a number of statements from Al Smith's speech, entitled "Betrayal of the Democratic Party," because it serves as an important historical record of the time when the Democrat Party abandoned capitalism and embraced socialism. (Al Smith's speech is printed in the Appendix of W. Cleon Skousen, *The Naked Capitalist* (Salt Lake City: W. Cleon Skousen, 1970), 122-129). Smith said:

> What are these dangers that I see? The first is the arraignment of class against class. . . .[T]here can be no permanent prosperity in this country until industry is able to employ labor, and there certainly can be no permanent recovery upon any governmental theory of "soak the rich."
>
> The next danger that is apparent to me is the vast building up of new bureaus of government, draining resources of our people in a common pool of redistributing them . . . .

Smith complained that Roosevelt had abandoned the Democrat platform, and had replaced it with socialist programs and principles. The abandoned planks include:

> First plank: "We advocate immediate and drastic reduction of governmental expenditures by abolishing useless commissions and offices, consolidating departments and bureaus, and eliminating extravagance to accomplish a saving of not less than 25 per cent in the cost of the Federal Government."
>
> Another plank: "We favor maintenance of the national credit

---

[26] "One of the greatest errors ever made by an American President occurred when Franklin D. Roosevelt [in 1933] extended diplomatic recognition to the godless Soviet conspiracy—after each of four American Presidents in succession had refused to do so" (Benson, *An Enemy*, 82).

by a Federal budget annually balanced . . . ."

Another one: "We promise the removal of Government from all fields of private enterprise except where necessary to develop public works and national resources in the common interest."

Here is another one: "We condemn the open and covert resistance of administrative officials to every effort made by congressional committees to curtail the extravagant expenditures of Government . . . ."

Smith expressed grave concern for the growing national debt. He said this:

> This debt is going to be paid by the great big middle class that we refer to as the backbone and the rank and file, and the sin of it is that they ain't going to know that they are paying it. It is going to come to them in the form of indirect and hidden taxation. It will come to them in the cost of living, in the cost of clothing, in the cost of every activity that they enter into, and because it is not a direct tax, they won't think they're paying, but, take it from me, they are going to pay it!

Smith concluded his analysis by stating that the current policies of the Roosevelt Administration are identical with the platform of the Socialist Party. Smith said: "Just get the platform of the Democrat Party, and get the platform of the Socialist Party, and lay them down . . . side by side." Smith said that the work of the Roosevelt Administration fulfilled the Socialist Party platform, but not the Democrat Party platform on which Roosevelt ran. Smith said: "[T]his is the first time that I have known a party, upon such a huge scale, not only not to carry out the plank, but to do the directly opposite thing to what they promised."

Smith finished his speech, calling upon Democrats and President Roosevelt to "[s]top attempting to alter the form and structure of our Government." Smith said the foremost of the principles of our government is that the federal government is "strictly limited in its powers" and that preserving such limitations is necessary "to insure State's rights, guarantee home rule, and preserve freedom of individual initiative and local control."

And lest there be any doubt that Smith was concerned that the new socialist programs threatened America to becoming too aligned with communism, Smith said: "There can be only one atmosphere of government, the clear, pure, fresh air of free America, or the foul breath of Communistic Russia." Al Smith's speech makes it pretty clear that the Roosevelt Administration established many socialistic programs in the federal government.[27]

Later Presidents and later Congresses passed laws and made changes to make America even more socialistic. The next major transformation took place as a part of Lyndon Johnson's "Great Society" in the mid-1960s. Socialist encroachment continued after that, and reached its most extensive expansion in 2010 by passage of the "Affordable Care Act," which was not affordable, but which established universal health care and mandatory taxation to make the citizens pay for it. We will discuss these changes shortly, but first let us review the era of heightened fear of communism infiltration in America in the early 1950s.

The height of opposition to communism is marked by the efforts of Senator Joseph McCarthy (R-WI) in the 1950s to identify and oust communists from the federal government. He identified a lot of people—so many that he ended up alienating almost everybody. The public and the press turned against him, which resulted in McCarthy being censured by the Senate—a very unusual and severe reprimand for McCarthy. "McCarthyism" is the word we use today to identify anti-communist fanatics. But there are respectable historians who believe McCarthy was mostly correct. The infestation of communist sympathizers had already become so extensive in the mid-1950s that

---

[27] Beginning in 1933, newly elected President Franklin D. Roosevelt established, with the almost complete cooperation of Congress, the following programs, many of which had substantial socialistic elements:

AAA	Agriculture Adjustment Agency (1933)
NRA	National Recovery Administration (1933)
PWA	Public Works Administration (1933)
CCC	Civilian Conservation Corps (1933)
FDIC	Federal Deposit Insurance Corporation (1933)
SEC	Securities and Exchange Commission (1934)
SSA	Social Security Administration (1935)
TVA	Tennessee Valley Authority (1933)
WPA	Works Progress Administration (1935)
REA	Rural Electrification Program (1935)
NLRB	National Labor Relations Board (1935)
FHA	Federal Housing Administration (1937)
FLSA	Fair Labor Standards Act (1938)
FS	Food Stamp Program (1939)

McCarthy became a fatality of the hands of the Deep State (the Establishment). Self-preservation led the socialists in government and in the media to turn on McCarthy and politically destroy him for challenging and threatening the socialists.

The McCarthy censure in 1954 inaugurated an increased acceptance of socialistic programs in America. This was the unintended but effectual result of extinguishing McCarthyism. The anti-McCarthy backlash was so strong that ever after it became totally unacceptable, both politically and socially, to accuse someone of being a communist or a socialist. Historically, the censure of McCarthy marked the high point of national opposition to communism. Immediately thereafter the people would hesitate before accusing anyone of being communist. The national reluctance to be too quick to attack communists has turned into a tolerance and acceptance of socialistic/communistic philosophies and policies.

B. Creeping Socialism

In the 1960s (especially in the Lyndon Johnson administration, through his "Great Society" and through "Civil Rights" legislation), Congress and the President enacted massive laws and governmental programs that were socialistic. In 1969, Ezra Taft Benson wrote: "[T]his present Congress has passed more socialistic legislation recommended by a president that probably any other Congress in the history of our Republic" (Benson, *An Enemy*, 309).

During the 1960s there were some who criticized these changes, but not with much success. For example, Senator Barry Goldwater (R-AZ, and Republican nominee for President in 1964) criticized some of this socialist encroachment, but he was attacked so relentlessly and effectively by the media, that he suffered one of the most lopsided defeats of all time in the 1964 presidential election; Lyndon Johnson was re-elected. Johnson's Great Society continued for another four years. But then widespread upset with the Vietnam conflict took over the political conversation in the 1968 election.

The political environment for Lyndon Johnson in 1964-1968 was similar to that which FDR enjoyed in the 1930s; Congress enacted almost every socialistic program that Johnson proposed, some of which were a part of his "War on Poverty." Consider the list of programs and enactments:

46

Community Action Agency
Head Start
Medicaid
Medicare
National Endowment for the Arts
Elementary and Secondary Education Act
Higher Education Act
Bilingual Education Act
Public Broadcasting Act
Fair Labor Standards Act
Economic Development Act
Cigarette Labeling and Advertising Act
Fair Packaging and Labeling Act
Wholesome Meat Act
Truth-in-Lending Act
National Highway Traffic Safety Administration
Endangered Species Preservation Act
National Environmental Policy Act
Clean Air Act
Civil Rights Act of 1964
Voting Rights Act of 1965

This is obviously an impressive list. Every one of these laws and programs brought good things to some people, but this represents a major transition in the purposes of our federal government, as it became the provider for citizens. By the enactment of these laws and programs, the federal government usurped control over things that had previously been matters of state, local or individual control—education, welfare, housing and health care. In addition, the federal government began to establish federal environmental laws and policies. Finally, passage of the Civil Rights Act and the Voting Rights Act provided federal regulation and remedies for various types of racial discrimination. Make no mistake, the "Great Society" wrought a major change in America's federal system—strengthening the power and dominion of the federal government, and diminishing States' rights and individual rights. Just reading the list of these many programs and enactments should make it obvious that they together represent a major adoption of socialist programs in America. Even the civil rights enactments included socialist elements.

Ezra Taft Benson warned that the "civil rights" movement was more about the advancement of socialist programs than about the protection of civil rights. He said: "The new 'civil rights' legislation is, I am convinced, about ten percent civil rights and about ninety percent a further extension of socialistic federal controls. It is a fraud. It is part of the pattern for the communist take-over of America. The whole 'civil rights' program and slogan in American today is just as phony as were the 'agrarian reform' program and slogan of the communists in China twenty years ago" (Benson, *An Enemy*, 109).

While increased socialism was being rolled out in the "Great Society," there were some strong voices who were warning America of this socialist encroachment, and who continued to sound the alarm of the encroachment of socialism and communism in America in the late 1950s and the 1960s: Milton Friedman, J. Edgar Hoover, W. Cleon Skousen, Ezra Taft Benson and David O. McKay are five influential people who continued to sound the alarm about the continuing threats of communism and socialism.

Senator Strom Thurmond identified and warned against what Benson calls "creeping socialism" (Newquist, 261) with these words: "Socialism can be brought about by government regulation, taxation, and control of property almost as effectively as by outright state ownership of the means of production and distribution."[28] Unfortunately, that is exactly what happened. In 1969, Ezra Taft Benson explained: "For thirty years we have aided the cause of the atheistic socialistic conspiracy by permitting socialists, communists, and fellow-travelers in high places in government; . . . by recklessly spending ourselves to near bankruptcy by weakening our free enterprise system through adoption of socialistic policies; . . . [and] by ever increasing confiscatory taxation" (Benson, *An Enemy*, 50).

In Benson's book, *An Enemy Hath Done This*, his main thesis is that "we [America] are at war with international communism which is committed to the destruction of our government, our right of property, and our freedom" (Benson, *An Enemy*, 144-45). Benson states: "I am unalterably opposed to socialism, either in whole or in part, and regard it as an unconstitutional usurpation of power and a denial of the right of private property for the government to own or operate the means of producing and distributing goods and services in competition with

---

[28] Sen. Strom Thurmond (1964), quoted in Benson, *An Enemy*, 20 and also 108-109.

private enterprise or to regiment owners in the legitimate use of private property. . . . [E]very person who enjoys the protection of life, liberty and property should bear his fair share of the cost of government in providing that protection" (Benson, *An Enemy*, 145).

C. Overt Socialism

The election of Barack Hussein Obama in 2008 marked a shift in American politics to an era where more and more candidates have campaigned overtly for America to embrace socialism. Many of Barack Obama's campaign proposals were certainly liberal, and I submit that they were socialistic. But Obama did not identify himself as a socialist. Obama represented the typical advocate of creeping socialism who did not want to be labeled a socialist. But Obama governed as a one-world socialist. He did not govern to the middle—reaching across the aisle for some measures, the way Bill Clinton did. Rather Obama governed far to the left, and he spoke fondly of socialism, and he apologized to nations around the world for America's being too rich and for causing many of the world's problems. Obama continued to move more and more to the left during his two terms. One telling aspect of the 2012 election campaign is characterized by Obama's criticizing American businesses and insisting that "you did not build it." The Republicans specifically disputed this, as their nominee, Mitt Romney, campaigned in support of America's free enterprise system, which Obama was criticizing.

One interpretation of Obama's victory over Romney in 2012 was that the nation was turning socialist. The reasons for Obama's re-election are more complicated than that, but the socialists were certainly emboldened. Then, in the 2016 Democrat presidential primaries, the Democrats featured a drawn-out two-man race between Hillary Clinton and the avowed socialist Bernie Sanders. Hillary Clinton ultimately prevailed in the Democrat primaries, but large support for an unabashed socialist was impressive and disconcerting. Socialism was gaining momentum in the Democrat Party. By the time we got to the 2020 presidential campaign, the Democrat Party produced over twenty socialist candidates. The initial leading Democrat candidate, Joe Biden, who was already much too liberal for the liking of Republicans, found himself being perhaps too conservative for the Democrat voters. The stage was set for Democrats to boldly campaign for socialist policies and programs. And that's what happened. See the next chapter.

CHAPTER SEVEN

SOCIALISM OF 2020 DEMOCRAT PRESIDENTIAL CANDIDATES

The socialist platforms of most of the Democrat Presidential candidates for the 2020 Election would destroy freedoms and hasten economic disaster for America.

In 2018, two years before the 2020 Presidential Election, over two dozen presidential campaigns were under way—most of them Democrat candidates. The two primary issues raised by the Democrats have been: (1) Get rid of Trump, and (2) Establish socialist programs. Much has been written about President Donald Trump, but this book will avoid discussing him, except as related to discussions of capitalism and socialism. Trump is a strong spokesman for capitalism, and so the socialist candidates oppose Trump's capitalism. In fact, I submit that it is in large measure because Trump is a fierce opponent of socialism that the Democrats continually smear and malign him with accusations unrelated to his economic philosophy. Part of the communist play book is to create discord, revolt, rioting, and name-calling, whenever possible. Making false accusations is always encouraged by socialists.[29]

American politics in 2019 is dominated by smears, name-calling and ad hominem attacks. Such attacks on President Donald Trump have been relentless. He is repeatedly called "racist," "fascist," "white

---

[29] Karl Marx said that violence and revolution are tools to be used to bring about the overthrow of government in order to establish communism. Skousen, 18 and 26. Lenin doubled down on this. He said: "[V]iolence will be an inevitable accompaniment of the collapse of capitalism." "Only insurrection can guarantee the victory of the revolution." "The purpose of insurrection must be, not only the complete destruction, or removal of all local authorities." V. I. Lenin, "Selected Works," Vol. III, pp. 315-316, 327 and 377, quoted in Skousen, 295, 296 & 297.

national supremacist," "liar," "mentally ill," "xenophobe," "Hitler," a "conspirator with Russia," "traitor," and a host of other derogatory labels.   Today, the hatred of Trump by the mainstream media and by many leading political leaders is so intense and relentless that it has been successful in silencing some people who support Trump, and it has short-circuited legitimate debate about many important issues. It is true that Trump himself has used name-calling, so it could be said that he is getting his just desserts. But the current political polarization in America has gone too far—it is now toxic. There must be a disciplined return to respectful debate about the issues of our day, or else America will suffer serious consequences of mob rule, rejection of the rule of law, and a democratic repudiation of American liberties.

In addition to smearing Trump, the Democrat presidential candidates of 2019 propose multiple socialist programs. Consider this list of socialist programs that they are promoting:

> Fight climate change
> Living wage
> Minimum wage
> Free health care
> Free college
> Reparations
> Increase taxes on wealthy
> Sanctuary cities
> No border walls
> Abolish ICE
> Free Stuff

As of this writing, the top three Democrat candidates fall into three separate camps: (1) Bernie Sanders is an avowed "socialist," and he proudly hails socialism as the panacea for all of America's problems and needs; (2) Elizabeth Warren and her proposals are just about as socialist as those of Bernie Sanders, except Warren insists she is not a "socialist," but is a "capitalist"; and (3) Joe Biden appears to be a moderate on economic issues (seen as the least socialist of the candidates). But Biden has been changing his views right and left during this campaign, as he attempts to adopt the views of the vocal, left-wing socialists who are stirring considerable activity among the Democrats. This presents an odd dilemma for the Democrats: Vote for an extremist "Socialist" (Bernie), OR vote for the phony Warren, who denies that she is a socialist, but is a socialist, OR vote for Joe Biden who seems to be more "socialist" every day, but who argues that he is the most electable Democrat because his positions are not so extreme. On the Republican side, all three of these are too socialist.

One interesting phenomenon of the current political scene is the fact that in 2019 the three Democrats that have gotten more air time than almost any other Democrats are the three freshmen Congresswomen: Alexandria Ocasio-Cortez (D-NY) [referred to as "AOC"], Ilhan Omar (D-MN) and Rashida Tlaib (D-MI). These three are commonly referred to as the "Squad" because they sometimes appear together at press conferences and other activities. They have distinguished themselves by how outspoken they have been in denigrating Trump and calling for his impeachment (which is always embraced with enthusiasm by the press) and by their outrageous and extreme proposals. AOC introduced the "Green New Deal," and Ilhan Omar (D-MN), and Rashida Tlaib (D-MI) have been overtly anti-Semitic. These three women have captured the attention of the media all year. Although their substantive positions are left of most Democrats, nevertheless they generate a lot of excitement and discussion. They are a thorn in the side of Speaker of the House Nancy Pelosi, as they continue to demand that Trump be impeached, which leaves Pelosi in the position of trying to keep the youngsters in the fold (so their votes will be there when needed), but not to allow their extremist demands to damage her party. But the "Squad" are also unabashed, insistent socialists. And in this respect, they represent the left wing of the Democrat Party, and those Democrats who are seeking their party's nomination are hoping to ride the coat tails of the energy produced by the Squad. There is considerable political power that is advancing socialism in America.

Meanwhile, back to the Democrat candidates. While all of them embrace many socialist programs, they nevertheless attempt to differentiate themselves from the communists in Russia, China and Cuba. They all take the implicit position that if the people vote for socialism then there can be nothing wrong with it. But this is not true. The communist countries all have elections. As Judge Jeanine Pirro said: "Socialism represents the worst aspect of democracy: the propensity for the majority to vote themselves the property of the minority" (Pirro, 218). This highlights the fact that the majority rule in democracy is not always good. Mob rule is one species of democracy that we acknowledge to be bad. And why is it bad—because we acknowledge in America that there are other individual rights that must be protected. These rights include due process rights, property rights, and freedom of speech rights. Thus, in America we recognize that something bad is not made right just because a majority of people may support it. And this is certainly the case with socialism; majority approval does not mean that socialism is good.

So, now, thirty years after the 1989 global repudiation of socialism, the socialists are back with a vengeance, openly decrying capitalism and calling for the United States to adopt the most extreme socialist programs and measures ever before suggested: Free college for all; free health care for all, including illegal aliens; a guaranteed living wage for all; increased taxation of the wealthy to pay for the increased entitlements promised to the poor and middle class; increased government control over all aspects of life that affect the environment or that are predicted to affect the environment.

This latter area is currently the poster child of socialism, as the socialist alarmists cry that climate change will bring about the destruction of the world in ten years if we do not immediately wean ourselves from fossil fuels, stop flying airplanes, and become a vegetarian world. Some Democrat candidates say that climate change is the biggest problem facing America today; they call it an "existential threat." AOC leads this charge, insisting that rising sea levels will ruin the world in ten years, unless we fix it. The socialist alarmists exaggerate the threats and risks, and they gullibly respond to every call of Chicken Little that the sky is falling, whether or not scientific facts really support such concerns. Those who question or dispute Chicken Little are demonized as ignorant and selfish and immoral. The militant socialists advocate a new morality that condemns and punishes those who dispute with Chicken Little. Climate change deniers are considered more immoral than hardened criminals. In fact, the Climate Change crowd advocates to give convicted felons the right to vote; and to give sanctuary to criminal, illegal aliens in America. The current environmentalists are one and the same as today's socialists.

Climate change is a hollow political slogan that is without supporting facts and reason. Climate change fanatics cannot tell you what specific effects their proposals will have on climate change. For example, if airplane travel is eliminated and if the eating of meat is outlawed, will this stop climate change. No, of course not. Okay, then is there any way to measure how this would lesson climate change? No.

Well, if this is the case, there will never be any way to know whether eliminating airplane travel and the eating of meat had any helpful effect.

This illustrates the problem with climate change proposals. There must be a comparison made of the cost-effectiveness of various proposals before an intelligent decision can be made as to how to best address climate change. It may very well be that it would be a waste of time to try to stop climate change, and that it would be best to come up with the most cost-effective way to cope with it, rather than waste efforts trying to stop it. If we think that rising seas will put a city under water, it may be better to move out of that city than to try to stop the seas from rising. If the temperatures are going to increase in an area, it may be better to develop strains of crops that will produce well in the warmer environment, than to attempt to stop global warming. As Milton Friedman explained forty years ago: "Even the most ardent environmentalist doesn't really want to stop pollution. If he thinks about it, and doesn't just talk about it, he wants to have the right amount of pollution. We can't really afford to eliminate it—not without abandoning all the benefits of technology that we not only employ but on which we depend."[30]

But even though the phrase "climate change" is too nebulous and vague to be connected with any specific proposal, it has nevertheless become the socialist banner to destroy capitalism. I mentioned earlier in the book that the "climate change" movement is as much a war on capitalism as a pro-environmental effort. The sub-title of Naomi Klein's book leaves no question that this is the case: "Capitalism vs. The Climate."

For those of you who doubt the inextricable connection between socialists and the climate change movement, you need to wake up and pay attention to what is unfolding before your eyes. On Friday, September 20, 2019, there was a world-wide "climate change" strike that involved 161 countries and involved demonstrations in 5,800 places around the world. I read that as many as 3 million people may have participated world-wide. The demonstrations were titled "youth climate strike," but those who observed what unfolded all know that the

---

[30] Milton Friedman, *There's No Such Thing as a Free Lunch*, quoted at https://www.goodreads.cvom/author/quotes/5001.Milton_Friedman, accessed September 9, 2019.

demonstrations were against capitalism as much as about climate change. Many of the signs displayed made this abundantly clear:

"Capitalism Is Evil"
"Capitalism Destroys Nature"
"Save the Planet from Capitalism"
"Capitalism Kills"
"System Change, Not Climate Change"

And if that is not enough to make it obvious that the "youth climate strike" was specifically against capitalism, you should see what the organizers and supporters said about capitalism. Writing about the "youth climate strike," *Los Angeles Times* opinion writer, Ian Haney Lopez, said this: "For groups like the Sunrise Movement, one of the climate strike's instigators, the demand for action on climate change can't be severed from the broad social justice framework of a Green New Deal."[31] The world-wide demonstrations on September 20th were openly supported and promoted by socialists. On September 21st, the lead article on the World Socialist Web Site was titled, "Millions march against climate change, capitalism and war."[32] A month before the demonstrations were to take place, "One Democracy" (another organization who promoted the world-wide demonstration) published an article on their web site: "The fight against climate change is a fight against capitalism."[33]

The socialists of 2019 march under the banner of "climate change." This was literally done on September 20, 2019, in the "Youth Climate Strike" marches around the world. Liberal educators around America supported a national skip school day, in order to support these marches, which are being done to highlight and support the United Nations' Climate Action Summit, which is to begin on September 23, 2019.

---

[31] Ian Haney Lopez, "Opinion: Why youth climate strike has to take on racial justice," *Los Angeles Times*, September 19, 2019.
https://www.latimes.com/opinion/story/2019-09-19/climate-strike-environment-racial-justice
[32] Bryan Dyne and Will Morrow, "Millions march against climate change, capitalism and war," September 21, 2010. https://www.wsws.ort/en/articles/2019/09/21/clim-s21/html
[33] Simon Hannah, "The fight against climate change is a fight against capitalism," August 13, 2019. https://www.opendemocracy.net/en/oureconomy/fight-against-climate-change-fight-against

But not only are these climate change demonstrations merely an arm of socialist propaganda, they are also made to look like the world's youth are spontaneously joining together to combat climate change. But the reality, is these youth are merely the pawns of the socialist pied pipers, who are using the youth for their political purposes. So the demonstrations present the theme: "The capitalists are denying climate change and destroying the planet." And thus, capitalism is the evil cause of climate change. And thus, establishing socialism is the cure for climate change; because when the government controls all the property, then the government can tell people what to do with all property and all wealth. No! Socialism will not stop climate change. Socialism will eliminate private property rights, and it will also destroy prosperity and freedom. And the climate will continue to regularly change, just as it has always done during all of the earth's existence.

It is not the purpose of this book to address the various complex issues related to climate change, except to make it clear that the people behind the "climate change" agenda are socialists. And the calls these people make to fight climate change are also calls to fight capitalism. Whatever changes society should make to help our environment should not be promoted at the expense of capitalism. Further, recognize that "climate change" initiative, events and demonstrations are almost always planned and led by socialists. I don't want to have anything to do with the socialists, because they seek to destroy the freedoms that make America prosperous.

The socialists blame capitalism for climate change, and their simplistic solution to fix climate change is to end capitalism and establish socialism. To the socialists, not only is capitalism bad—it is evil! And the socialists go on from there to establish a new "morality," that whatever attacks capitalism is good. The socialists have embraced "the end justifies the means" morality, which, of course, is the very absence of morality.

Every four years, the American stage affords the opportunity for socialist extremists to conduct campaigns to cause America to reject capitalism and embrace socialism. A democratic republic has the built-in communication system that tolerates socialism, and gives it center stage to repeatedly attempt to convince the voters to embrace the false security it promises and to sacrifice freedoms to reach this nirvana. Thus, we must repeatedly address the socialist threat. And our national education system has now become infected with brain-washed, pseudo-intellectuals that are full-fledged socialists. Together, all of this presents a formidable threat to freedom, including a threat to our free-market capitalist economy and the prosperity it facilitates.

These socialists are embodied in over a dozen Democrat candidates for their party's nomination for President. There's a good chance that one of them will be that nominee, and this is a scary thought. And, thus the need for this book. I hope this book helps, and I hope it's not too late.

CONCLUSION

Every voting citizen in America needs to have a basic understanding of the differences between capitalism and socialism. Everyone needs to know that capitalism promotes both freedom and prosperity, but that socialism is an economic system that restricts freedoms with the fraudulent promise that it will bring the people security and prosperity. The fraud is that it does not and cannot bring prosperity. Every voter needs to understand this. Those who do understand will support candidates who are capitalists, and they will reject the candidates who proclaim themselves to be "socialist" as well as the candidates whose platforms support socialistic programs (whether or not they admit to being socialist).

Two of the most effective voices in the 1960s and 1970s who warned against the dangers of creeping socialism, as well as the overt threats of communism were Ezra Taft Benson and W. Cleon Skousen. I have included in this book multiple statements from these men because they were both articulate and prescient in describing the threats and dangers of communism and socialism. But the world has been significantly re-shaped in the fifty years after they published their books. Benson and Skousen were proven right in 1989 when there was a world-wide repudiation of communism as more than a dozen communist economies collapsed that year. This brought many nations to embrace free-market capitalism at that time. The establishment of capitalism and the free enterprise system is indeed the best way to both prosperity and freedom, but prosperity still requires work and diligence and patience.

But capitalism is not exempt from economic downturns and weather and war and innovation and technological developments that can disrupt and otherwise affect both individuals and nations. Consequently, since the major international embracement of capitalism in 1989, many nations and peoples have once again been enticed to follow the siren call of socialism, as Judge Jeanine Pirro describes in her recent book (Pirro,209-210). If America is lured by the siren calls of socialism, and then elects socialists and enacts increasingly socialist laws, then we will reap the reward of loss of liberty and economic disaster. A wise and informed America will reject socialism and the damage it always brings.

APPENDIX A.

SERIOUS PROBLEMS WITH THE UNITED NATIONS

One of the stated objectives of Marx, Lenin and Stalin was to create a one-world, communist government. In 1945, immediately after World War II, the nations of the world formed the United Nations, and put its headquarters in the United States. The communists have been more than happy to participate in the U.N. and to use it for their purposes. Although the stated purposes of the U.N. did not call for the creation of a one-world government, the operations of the UN certainly have provided an avenue for this. But the U.N. was not established with the same framework for liberties, rights and governmental limitations that are secured by the U. S. Constitution. Because of this, a global government by the U.N. would be a disaster. Thus, maintaining the independence and sovereignty of America must not be sacrificed by participation in the U.N.

But not all Americans share this view. Benson said that some of our leaders have been more concerned with world opinion "than they are with securing the best possible advantage for us," and that "they are willing to sacrifice narrow American interests for the greater good of the community" (Benson, *An Enemy*, 205). Benson criticized this anti-nationalist attitude which has led some to regard "[p]atriotism and America-first" as "vulgar concepts" (*Id.*). Benson said this in 1969. This debate continues in 2019.

Through its various agencies, the U.N. has made proposals for setting prices, production quotas, labor standards, wages, and monetary standards (Benson, *An Enemy*, 205). But the U.N. has also supported world-wide abortion advocacy and diminishing parental rights in the rearing of their children.[34] The U.N. is also a leading advocate for world-

---

[34] Two popular U.N. conventions (i.e., treaties) have supported some world-wide initiatives that have several serious weaknesses: The Convention on the Rights of the Child (CRC) and the Convention on the Elimination of All Forms of Discrimination Against Women (CEDAW). The title of these two conventions sounds good, but the substance of each has serious problems. The CEDAW was adopted by the U.N. in 1979; the CRC was adopted by the UN in 1989. Neither of these has been approved by the Senate, so they are not legally binding in the U.S. Both the CRC and the CEDAW share some common flaws: they pit parents against children, make the government guardian of the children, promote abortion, and prohibit all gender discrimination. In addition, the CEDAW attacks the role of mothers in the family, legalizes prostitution, and attacks the free

wide climate change initiatives. The Kyoto Protocol of 1997 and the Paris Agreement of 2015 were both proposed by the U.N., which continues to be an advocate of climate change initiatives, some of which are of disputed need and value. In addition, the impact of these agreements on the U.S. is regarded by some as being unfair, unwarranted and punitive.

Benson said that "[e]very conceivable sphere of human activity is being analyzed and then planned for so that it will come under the ultimate control of the United Nations. It is becoming a world legislature, world court, world department of education, world welfare agency, world planning center for industry, science and commerce, world finance agency, world police force, and world anything else anyone might want—or might not want" (Benson, *An Enemy*, 205). "Nothing in the Constitution grants that the President shall have the privilege of offering himself as a world leader. He is our executive; he's on our payroll, . . . ; he's supposed to put our best interests in front of those of other nations" (Benson, *An Enemy*, 151).

Advocates for a world government criticize those who promote nationalism and putting America first. Ezra Taft Benson said that such criticisms are "utter nonsense":

> What kind of logic assumes that loving one's country means jealousy, suspicion and hatred of all others? Why can't we be proud of America as an independent nation and also have a feeling of brotherhood and respect for other peoples around the world? As a matter of fact, haven't Americans done just that for the past 200 years? What people have poured out more treasure to other lands, opened their doors to more immigrants, and sent more missionaries, teachers and doctors than we? Are we now to believe that love or our own country will suddenly cause us to hate the peoples of other lands? (Benson, *An Enemy*, 155-156)

President Herbert Hoover said that nationalism is a "great spiritual force." He said that "[t]he fuzzy-minded intellectuals have sought to brand nationalism as a sin against mankind. They seem to think that infamy is attached to the word 'nationalist'." But they are wrong. "The spirit of nationalism springs from the deepest of human emotions. It rises from the yearning of men to be free of foreign

---

enterprise system. This latter attack is done by requiring equal pay for men and women without regard to the quality and quantity of work performed. See C. Paul Smith, *The State of the Constitution—2017*, pp. 59-64.

domination, to govern themselves" (Herbert Hoover, quoted in Benson, 155-156). Theodore Roosevelt said that "it is only the man who ardently loves his country first who in actual practice can help any other country at all" (Benson, *An Enemy*, 156).

There are certainly some good reasons to create an organization to foster communication and cooperation between the many different nations in the world. But if too much is attempted to be accomplished through such a world organization there would be and are many pitfalls and dangers in such an organization. This is certainly the case with the United Nations. Such problems in the U.N. appeared from its very beginning, and astute observers have pointed them out. Ezra Taft Benson said that "the concept woven into all of the present-day proposals for world government (the U.N. foremost among these) is one of unlimited governmental power to impose by force a monolithic set of values and conduct on all groups and individuals whether they like it or not" (*Id.*, 160). In 1945, J. Reuben Clark voiced this concern about the newly formed United Nations: "The Charter certainly will not end war. . . . It is true the charter provides for force to bring peace, but such use of force is itself war. . . . It is true the Charter is built to prepare for war, not to promote peace. . . . The Charter is a war document not a peace document. . . . " (*Id.*).

The creation of the United Nations was intended to protect the world from oppression, but the U.N. has incorporated many socialistic policies and programs that restrict and diminish freedoms. Thus, while the U.N. has provided some benefits, it has also become an instrument of socialism. "Whereas the United States is founded on the concept of limited government, the U.N. concept is one of unlimited government power with virtually no meaningful restraints to protect individual liberty" (*Id.*, 204). "[T]he U.N.'s potential for evil far outweighs its potential for good" (*Id.,* 202).

How could the U.N. not have serious problems when many of the 120 plus nations in the U.N. are military dictatorships? What type of policing can we expect from the U.N. when from 1945-1970, every head of the U.N. forces (Undersecretary General for Political and Security Council Affairs) was selected from the Soviet Union (*Id.*, 179-180). "Allowing members of the world's greatest peace-destroying force to help a "peacekeeping" organization makes about as much sense as appointing members of the Mafia to a police commissioner's board to control crime in Chicago!" (*Id.*, 207). What kind of human rights protection and encouragement can you expect from a Human Rights Council composed of the leaders from Russia, China, Cuba and Saudi Arabia?[35]

One of the problems with the U.N. is that America's protection of the U.N. has allowed for Soviet agents to enter and operate in America with impunity. Multiple times in the 1960s, FBI Director J. Edgar Hoover testified before Congressional hearings that:

> the U.N. is not merely an occasional haven for a Soviet agent, but is, in fact, the *center* of communist espionage in America! The diplomatic immunity afforded to these people due to their U.N. status automatically protects them against arrest for violating the laws of this country. In other words, these communist espionage agents at the U.N. are above the law! . . . Diplomatic immunity also prevents customs officials from inspecting the personal baggage of these espionage agents. How convenient for them! How idiotic for us!" (Benson, *An Enemy*, 205-206)

The point is that the U.N. is no talisman to cure the world's problems. It does provide a forum where international leaders can meet and address common concerns. But the U.N. Charter and many of its programs conflict with the U. S. Constitution and our capitalist, free-market economy. The U.N. has become an antagonist to full freedom and human rights. Therefore, we must beware of U.N. programs and policies.

---

[35] The U.N.'s Human Rights Council is comprised of leaders from 47 nations, the selection of which rotates from year to year. From 2014-2016, Russia, China, Cuba and Saudi Arabia were on this council.

APPENDIX B.

LATTER-DAY SAINT ISSUES WITH SOCIALISM

In Nauvoo, in September of 1843, Joseph Smith listened to two lectures about socialism from a man named Mr. Finch. After the lecture was over, Joseph wrote: "I told them that I did not believe the doctrine" (*History of the Church*, 6:33). It was four years later, in 1847, when Karl Marx and Friedrich Engels published their *Manifesto*, which included a succinct statement about the objectives of communism. A few years after this, in 1859, Charles Darwin published his theory about natural selection. These two theories/movements have resulted in major changes in the world. Interestingly, both Marx and Darwin began to draw many atheistic followers. In 1882, President John Taylor said this: "Besides the preaching of the Gospel, we have another mission, namely, the perpetuation of the free agency of man and maintenance of liberty, freedom and the rights of man" (*Journal of Discourses*, 23:63). Ezra Taft Benson said that President Taylor's statement applies to the Church's mission to uphold our Constitutional freedoms and to reject communism (Benson, *An Enemy*, 292). In 1936, The First Presidency (Pres. Heber J. Grant, J. Reuben Clark and David O. McKay) issued the following warning about communism:

> With great regret we learn from credible sources . . . that a few Church members are joining directly or indirectly, the communists and are taking part in their activities. . . .
>
> But communism is not a political party nor a political plan under the Constitution; it is a system of government that is the opposite of our Constitutional government, and it would be necessary to destroy our government before communism could be set up in the United States. . . . [T]o support communism is treasonable to our free institutions, and no patriotic American citizen may become either a Communist or supporter of Communism. (Benson, *An Enemy,* 347)

In 1966, President David O. McKay said this about communism and socialism:

> The position of this Church on the subject of communism has never changed. We consider it the greatest Satanical threat to peace, prosperity, and the spread of God's work among men that exists on the face of the earth. . . .
>
> We, therefore, commend and encourage every person and

every group who are sincerely seeking to study Constitutional principles and awaken a sleeping and apathetic people to the alarming conditions which are rapidly advancing about us. We wish all of our citizens throughout the land were participating in some type of organized self-education in order that they could better appreciate what is happening and know what they can do about it. . . .

No member of the church can be true to his faith, nor can any American be loyal to his trust, while lending aid, encouragement, or sympathy to any of these false philosophies; for if he does, they will prove snares to his feet." (Benson, *An Enemy*, 297)

Ezra Taft Benson amplified this warning: "No true Latter-day Saint and no true American can be a socialist or a communist or support programs leading in that direction. These evil philosophies are incompatible with . . . the true gospel of Jesus Christ" (Newquist, 261).

The battle between capitalism and socialism is merely a modern version of the eternal debate that Satan waged in the pre-earth spirit world, where he (Lucifer) insisted that his plan of equality was better than God's plan of freedom and opportunity. Lucifer insisted that he could save everybody, whereas he pointed out that God's plan would result in some people not returning to live with God. Lucifer insisted that his plan was better because he could save everybody, so that not a single soul would be lost. But Lucifer's plan was a fraud; it would not save anybody because without the freedom to choose—without the freedom to decide what we would or would not do—there would be no growth and no real success. Consequently, Satan's plan would save no one. No one would grow. Force would ensure equality of outcome. But force does not allow for the exercise of choice, and it does not allow for the law of the harvest to exist. Lucifer's plan sounds attractive to the ignorant, the lazy and the indolent. But it is philosophically and logically flawed. It could never allow for individual growth and happiness. Satan's plan is nothing more than forced equality, but without joy and happiness. Conversely, God's plan of happiness requires that we have the opportunity to succeed or to fail. The way to happiness requires living with the risk of failure and unhappiness. But the plan is perfectly fair. And it is the only way to growth and happiness.

Meanwhile, back on earth, socialists basically preach the same plan that led Lucifer and a third of the hosts of heaven to be cast out of

God's presence before this world began. This eternal battle continues to be waged here on earth.

In the 1950s and 1960s leaders of The Church of Jesus Christ of Latter-day Saints made a concerted effort to denounce communism and to warn its members and the world of the on-going threat of a communist infiltration of America's government. However, I am not aware of the Church's continuing such warnings after the death of President David O. McKay in 1970. To the best of my knowledge, even Ezra Taft Benson, who was an outspoken critic of communist and socialist encroachment in the 1950s and 1960s, and who was Prophet and President from 1985-1994, did not make such warnings during his presidency.

It is my observation that in recent years the Church has declined to speak out against the dangers of socialism. The Church never renounced its previous warnings, so there is no basis to think that it sought to correct or modify those warnings. There was a broad-based, world-wide rejection of communism in 1989, when the Soviet Union dissolved. For a period of time thereafter, the overt threat from communism did not seem significant. Of course, the highly visible failure of communism in 1989 did not hinder the vines of creeping socialism from continuing to extend their tentacles into other governments of the world. So the need to eradicate socialistic elements from governments around the world continues to exist. But since the Church is a world church, it may be best not to speak against the form of government of the countries into which it seeks to send missionaries— because some of these countries are overtly socialist or communist, and many others have become de facto socialist countries. I submit that the Church has decided to avoid talking about the evils of socialism so as not to create barriers to its mission to declare the gospel to all the world.

Nevertheless, Church leaders have left intact their admonition for members to independently act and speak to promote the principles of freedom. In 1961, Elder Ezra Taft Benson said in General Conference that a priesthood holder "should not wait for the Lord's servants to give instruction for every detail once they have announced the direction in which the priesthood should go. Each member should exercise prayerful judgment and then act. . . . [H]e should use his influence in the community . . . . He should use the political party of his choice to express his evaluation of important issues. He should see that his party is working to preserve freedom, not destroy it."[36]

A. The United Order

In the 1830s, in Kirtland, Ohio (just east of Cleveland), the followers of Joseph Smith practiced a type of communal living where there was significant sharing of wealth, and where they sought to live as the early disciples of Christ, who "had all things common" (Acts 4:32). They called this economic system the Law of Consecration and Stewardship, or the United Order.

The United Order is not the same thing as communism. There are some similarities, but the differences are very significant. First, under the United Order people owned real and personal property, and they had the right to keep the profits of their labors. This is a profound difference. Second, participation in the United Order was voluntary. Finally, worshipping God is the foundation of the participation in the United Order, while communism repudiates all religion.

The United Order was neither communism nor socialism. In 1936, The First Presidency explained the following: "Communism is not the United Order, and bears only the most superficial resemblance thereto; Communism is based upon intolerance and force, the United Order upon love and freedom of conscience and action; Communism involves forceful despoliation of confiscation, the United Order voluntary consecration and sacrifice" (Benson, *An Enemy*, 347-348).

Ezra Taft Benson explained that ["]Communism debases the individual and makes him the enslaved tool of the state, to which he must look for sustenance and religion. Communism destroys man's God-given free agency" (*Id.*, 351).

John Widtsoe explained that communism, socialism, fascism and Nazism "are all the same in essential theory" (Widtsoe, 304). He said that they all "oppose religion," "reject Christian morality," "prohibit free speech and action; eliminate private ownership and initiative; hold without exception the state above the individual" . . . . "The free agent has no place in their systems. . . . Force and terrorism are their weapons" (*Id.*, 304-305). Conversely, Widtsoe explained that

---

[36] Ezra Taft Benson, CR 10/61:69-75, quoted in Newquist, 262.

in the United Order, once the individual is given his "inheritance," that that property "is his very own; it is private property. This 'inheritance' he is free to use as he chooses. His free agency is carefully guarded. . . . He is under one obligation only: to be loyal to the order and to be wise and industrious in the use of the 'portion' given him" (*Id.*, 302). The individual's duty to the order means returning the surplus to the common treasury" (*Id.*, 303). In other words, the individual has discretion with regard to what his surplus is, what he should retain for his needs and purposes, and how much to contribute to the Order. Thus, in the United Order ownership of private property is recognized, as well as freedom to control one's own property.

BIBLIOGRAPHY

Benson, Ezra Taft, *An Enemy Hath Done This* (Salt Lake City: Parliament Publishers, 1969, 1994).

_____, *The Red Carpet* (Salt Lake City: Bookcraft, 1962, 1963).

"Crimes of Khrushchev against the Ukrainian People." (n.d.) In *Wikipedia*. Retrieved September 4, 2019, citing www.ukrweekly.com > old > archives. The archived article is from The Ukraine Weekly, September 17, 1960, by Dr. Lev E. Dobriansky and several others.

Friedman, Milton, *Capitalism and Freedom* (Illinois: Univ. of Chicago Press, 1962).

Journal of Discourses (26 vols.) (Liverpool, 1883)

Klein, Naomi, *This Changes Everything—Capitalism vs. Climate Change* (New York: Simon & Schuster, 2014)

Newquist, Jerreld L., *Prophets, Principles and National Survival* (Salt Lake City: Publishers Press, 1964, 1976).

Norberg, Johan, *In Defense of Global Capitalism* (Sweden: Timbro, 2001).

Pirro, Jeanine, *Radicals, Resistance, and Revenge—The Left's Plot to Remake America*
(New York: Center Street, Hatchett Book Group, 2019).

Posner, Richard A., *A Failure of Capitalism* (Cambridge, MA: Harvard University Press, 2009).

"Red Terror." (n.d.) In *Wikipedia*. Retrieved September 4, 2019.

Richards, Stephen L., *The Church in War and Peace* (Salt Lake City: Deseret Book Co., 1943).

Roberts, B. H., ed., *History of The Church of Jesus Christ of Latter-day Saints* (7 vols.) (Salt Lake City: Deseret Book Co., 1902, 1951).

Skousen, W. Cleon, *The Naked Capitalist* (Salt Lake City: W. Cleon Skousen, 1970, 1971).

_____, *The Naked Communist* (Salt Lake City: The Ensign Publishing Company, 1958, 1962).

Smith, C. Paul, *The State of the Constitution—2017* (Frederick, MD: C. Paul Smith, 2017).

"Stalin, Joseph." (n.d.) In *Wikipedia*. Retrieved September 4, 2019.

Widtsoe, John A., *Evidences and Reconciliations* (Salt Lake City: Bookcraft, 1943).

Wrightstone, Gregory, *Inconvenient Facts* (USA: Silver Crown Productions, LLC, 2017).

INDEX

Printed in Great Britain
by Amazon

20227713R10047